STORAGE

Sei.

SEP 1 2 1995

LAST OF THE FREE

LAST OF THE FREE

Gareth Patterson

St. Martin's Press
New York

Library of Congress Cataloging-in-Publication Data

Patterson, Gareth
The last of the free : an inspirational story of three young lions restored
to the wild, and the man who risked his life to protect them / Gareth
Patterson.
    p.   cm.
"A Thomas Dunne book."
ISBN 0-312-13109-7
1. Lions—Botswana. 2. Wildlife reintroduction—Botswana.
3. Patterson, Gareth, 1963-   . I. Title.
QL737.C23P369   1995
599.74'428—dc20   95-3765   CIP

First published in Great Britain by Hodder & Stoughton

First U.S. Edition: May 1995
10 9 8 7 6 5 4 3 2 1

The life of clouds is a parting and a meeting. A tear and a smile.
Kahlil Gibran, *A Tear and a Smile*

For Julie, with love and gratitude,
and in memory of a son, though not of my blood, but a son
to me in spirit.

. . . love knows not its own depth until the hour of separation.
Kahlil Gibran, *The Prophet*

ACKNOWLEDGEMENTS

Between 1989 and 1991, the first years of *Last of the Free*, many people, in so many ways, contributed to our work with the lions in the Tuli bushlands. Not all can be acknowledged here – but they know who they are.

Firstly, I wish to thank the Deputy Director of the Department of Wildlife and National Parks in Botswana, Mr L. Nchunga, and the Director of Kenya's Wildlife Service, Dr Richard Leakey, for supporting the relocation of Batian, Furaha and Rafiki. Additionally, I wish to thank Tuli Safari Lodge and the Elsa Trust for their important initial funding for the project. My appreciation goes to Kenya Airways and Air Botswana for their marvellous contribution.

In Kenya, I wish to thank Major Douglas Tatham Collins, Joe and Simone Cheffings of Bateleur Safaris, Monty Ruben, Sam Ngethe, Dr John Jonyo, Dr Dieter Rottcher and Rick Matthews for their great support during the time of the lions' move to Botswana.

In the Botswana Tuli bushlands I thank those landowners who support our work. Charter Reserve's warden, Bruce Petty, John Louw and Paul Otterman, all the officials at the Pont Drift borderpost, particularly Bane Sesa, Jerry, Godfrey, Gaborone and Mr 'Cold Beer', whose kindness in lending me his shotgun literally saved my life – this though is yet another story still to be told. To Inspector Nxane for the use of his rifle I too owe my thanks. I wish to thank all the game guides of the bushlands, particularly David Marupane, who, sometimes under difficult circumstances, were so free with information on the Tuli lions and voluntarily acted as my eyes and ears. I owe thanks to Alpheus Marupane for being so kind in the frequent times of mechanical disaster – and to Jippy and the many other inhabitants of the Tuli bushlands with whom I share friendship. I thank the honourable James Maruatona, MP, for his support and fairness, and Minister Ray Molomo. Additionally, I wish to thank the following: my mother and father for their support; Tuli Safari

Area's warden, David Mupungu; Mr Pangeti of Zimbabwe Parks; all members of the Zimbabwe Hunters' Association for what they did; Game Warden, Peter Senamolela; Mafika Manyatsa and the Tuli Lion Trust anti-poaching team; Salmon Maoma; Mary Kalikawe; Rory Bennett and Alida of Van & Truck Hire; John and Sarah Dewar; John Hunt and Reg Lascaris of Hunt Lascaris TBWA; John Sampson and Di Perry; Dr Andrew McKenzie; Christel de Wit; Nikki Moore; Inge Lederthell; Brian Jackman; Peter Rabuthu; the trustees of the Tuli Lion Trust; Patricia McCracken and *Personality* magazine; Penguin Books for the quote from Kuki Gallmann's book, *I Dreamed of Africa*; Leanne Wright of Sampson, Okes, Higgins, Chapman inc; and many others.

Lastly, I thank Rozanne Savory for all her tireless support, my agent, Tony Peake, and my editor, Humphrey Price, for their enthusiasm and belief in *Last of the Free*.

Photo Credits

'Andrew operated on Batian' – Phil Kahn

'Gareth and George' – Doddie Edmonds

'The lions would be filled with a sense of fun and excitement which was infectious' – Bruce Petty

All other photographs by Julie Davidson and Gareth Patterson.

PROLOGUE

'Mbatian', Mount Kenya's highest peak, points heavenwards, above slopes of stone and snow. Its twin, another great peak, is known as 'Nelion'. These towering mountainheads were named after two celebrated Masai brothers, both of whom were 'laibons' (clairvoyants, masters of religious ceremonies) and chieftains and lived a hundred years ago. To the north of these highlands is a place of hot days and cool nights – the Frontier District – and there, five years ago, lived a lioness with no name.

This lioness had been courted by and had mated with a large male whose mane was yellow, brown and gold, the colours of the wilderness, and life was conceived within her. Weeks passed after their couplings until one day, sensing that the time of birth was near, the lioness sought a hidden nursery site. There, alone in a place facing Mount Kenya, she gave birth to three cubs, three cubs whose lives I was later to share, whose lives became merged with my own.

It is their story I am about to tell. The story of Batian and his sisters, Furaha and Rafiki – the last of the free.

LAST OF THE FREE

INTRODUCTION

> We should not have to place a value on animals to
> whom values are unknown; we should be able to
> guarantee their freedom solely for their own sake,
> but man's thinking has only just begun to approach
> such a level of morality.
>
> George Schaller

The land in which the lioness lived was not a national park but a wild region of Kenya where cattle ranching and tourism based on wildlife have a somewhat unusual coexistence, operating side by side. Here the lioness hunted, preying upon zebras, eland, kongoni, impala, greater kudu, Grant's gazelle, gerenuk – and cattle.

The Craigs, a white Kenyan family with both tourism and cattle-ranching interests in this area, described her as a 'persistent stock killer'. Reluctant to destroy the lioness, the Craigs initially attempted to capture her alive and relocate her to a national park, thus curbing their losses and ensuring that she lived. Their attempts to 'boxtrap' her though were unsuccessful. Time passed and cattle continued to be killed.

This dilemma – a conflict between man and the continent's great predators so tragically typical of today's Africa – ultimately results in the continued demise of forms of life belonging to an older world, more complete than our own.

Early one morning, as pangs of hunger stirred within her, the lioness rose slowly from where she had been nursing the three cubs. After stretching her body she slipped out of the nursery site and moved away. The cubs sensed her absence and crawled to huddle together in a small, tawny heap. Instinctively they became quiet and, between slumbers, awaited the return of their mother to whom they had been born just five days before. Their mother never did return. They never again knew her, nor suckled for her rich milk, nor felt again her tongue caressing their mottled backs and creamy bellies.

That early morning their mother sought prey on the plains, seeking to fuel her body and in turn fuel those little forms, the future, hidden in the tawny grasses. Later she killed and began to eat a cow, her actions dictated by the symbiotic cycles of death and life. In man's eyes, so removed from these cycles, she had committed a crime, a crime against man's principal values of ownership, possession . . .

The lioness with no name was shot dead that day. The cattle killing, it had been decided, could no longer be afforded and therefore allowed to persist. After the shooting, as her golden form stiffened, it was discovered that she had been suckling young. The Craigs organised a search, saddened that their actions had resulted in the cubs now being without a mother. Two days later the nursery site was finally discovered. Batian, Furaha and Rafiki were found. Their eyes had just begun to open, they were unharmed and in surprisingly good condition.

The Craigs cared for the cubs for ten days before flying two hundred and fifty kilometres east with them to the Kora National Reserve. There, they gave the cubs to an old man with a mane of white hair, perhaps the only man who could strive to ensure that their future would not be one of imprisonment and cages, but a future of rightful freedom. The old man was George Adamson.

The tiny cubs were to become the last of the free, the last of a long line of lions cared for by George. The first of the free was the lioness Elsa, who had been returned back in 1956 to the wilds by George and his wife, Joy. With Elsa, the *Born Free* era began. *Born Free* is perhaps the most well-known and loved story of an animal that shared its life in the wilds not only with its own kind, but also with man. Joy Adamson wrote her best-selling trilogy, *Born Free, Living Free* and *Forever Free*, stories that touched the hearts of millions and in turn created an attitude of compassion and concern for Africa's wildlife.

Largely out of the limelight, George tirelessly continued to return a total of twenty-five lions back into the wilds over a period of almost thirty years. Today, descendants of these rehabilitated lions roam the Kora and Meru game reserves, lions he told me of like Growe and her pride.

The old man lived for the freedom of lions. He was often criticised by conservationists for his work, which they termed as 'unscientific' and 'of no value to conservation'. His critics missed the fundamental point, lacking George's wisdom and vision. His work was never intended to be a scientific quest but a work the essence of which was a strong moral issue.

George enabled lions to have the fundamental right to be free. Freedom, whether in the guise of the abolition of slavery in the past or the pursuance of human rights today, lies in the very fabric of man's being. George, long before the days of animal rights activism, believed that freedom was essential to all life, and he believed in a kinship with all life. He once wrote:

> *A lion is not a lion if it is only free to eat, to sleep and to copulate. It deserves to be free, to hunt and to choose its own prey, to look for and find its own mate, to fight for and hold its own territory, to die where it was born – in the wild. It should have the same rights as we have.*

Through my reading of George and Joy's books and articles on their work, George had been an inspiration to me from the time that I was a young boy growing up in Nigeria and Malawi, and had a strong influence on the course which my life took. By coincidence, I first met George just weeks before the cubs were given to him. I had visited Kora while researching material for my second book, *Where the Lion Walked*, a book concentrating on the past status and present plight of these animals; the focus of my life was the lion too.

I returned to Kora to assist George with his work two months after our first meeting. Naturally, upon arriving at his camp, 'Kampi ya Simba', I was eager, out of curiosity and concern, to see the three cubs for the first time. They and their situation symbolised the essence of the Adamson philosophy. George had named the little male Batian after 'Mbatian', the mountain peak near where he was born, and the two females Rafiki and Furaha, meaning 'friend' and 'joy' in Swahili.

I walked into the lion enclosure and peered into the shade of a large wooden crate. The three tiny cubs moved their heads, sensing my presence, but seemingly too young to focus their eyes on me. They were, of course, completely endearing and yet I felt saddened by seeing them. Although with George they had the best possible foster parent, I could not help but imagine them, as I knew he did too, in a shady nursery site in the wilds beside their mother. It was at that point, to me at least, that these three lions began to represent all of their persecuted kind.

Additionally, the baby lions stirred within me questioning thoughts about time and the future. The cubs would grow quickly, their instincts progressing with their physical development. They would become lions, members of their kind, who today increasingly, because of man's numbers and expansion, live upon restricted African plains. Standing there, looking at them, I could not help but ponder on their future. I then understood that such thinking was, in reality, a pointless exercise; only time would unveil their true future.

Today, I realise that the thoughts of 'time' and 'their future' which so filled my mind as I watched the cubs that day arose from my fear for them – a fear for all of their kind. At that time, a horrific situation was affecting wildlife and people at Kora and throughout Kenya. 'Shifta', Somali poachers, were devastating Kenya's elephant herds. In one national park alone, six hundred elephants were slaughtered in a six-month period. Kora's last herds also fell victim to the poachers' guns.

People too were tragically affected by the heavily armed gangs of Somalis. Busloads of passengers in remote areas were robbed and, on some occasions, shot dead. On the second day after my return to Kora, two rangers were killed in the reserve after their vehicle was ambushed – a third man, a survivor of the incident, was brought to George's camp with a bullet lodged in his back. It was a volatile time in Kora and in many parts of the country.

After the Kora ambush incident, Kenya's President Daniel arap Moi proclaimed a shoot-on-sight policy. Any unauthorised armed person resisting arrest in a wildlife area would be shot. In the months ahead, seventy 'shifta' in total – all of Somalia origin – were killed and as a result of this, a calm settled in the wildlife parks of Kenya.

It was during these times that I stayed with George at Kora for six months. He wished me to work with him and after him, to see that his work continued and Kora did not collapse in the future. It was an immense honour that George had bestowed upon me; but it was not, though, fated to be. Until Kora was upgraded to national park status, essential funding to implement conservation projects which I had planned with George would not be forthcoming. Without these two interlinked factors, no full-time role could be established for me at Kora.

I left Kora and all it held with a heavy heart in January 1989, and returned to southern Africa and began to write *The Lions' Legacy*, a book about George, a book for Kora. Its contents, I hoped, would contribute to the protection of that wild region and the old man's cause.

During that period, I also planned the re-establishment of my own lion study in the Botswana Tuli bushlands, a land where my love and concern for the African lion had been born six years previously. Increasingly I had come to realise that I had to continue to publicise the continental plight of the lion and in turn promote awareness and public consciousness of the issue. However, I needed, at the same time, to concentrate on the protection of a single threatened lion population and in turn to protect a single wilderness. I planned to return to the Tuli bushlands, and so I set about establishing a trust fund dedicated to the greater protection of the Tuli lions and their bushlands home. In time, with other objectives being drawn up, the Tuli Lion Trust was founded.

The news I received from Kora at this time was blessedly positive. In one of his newsletters, dated March 1989, George wrote the following:

> Security within the reserve is being maintained to a high standard and there is talk of a temporary police camp being made a more permanent fixture (in the reserve). Discussion continues on the subject of Kora being made a National Park which would stabilise its future – something I would dearly like to see happen. Currently we have no Somalis in the reserve and animals are noticeably less timid.
>
> The picture below [it shows George, wine glass in hand, standing with the three cubs beside a champagne bottle in a silver bucket] was taken on my 83rd birthday, 3rd February – the cubs seemed to take a liking to the champagne!

He finished the letter:

> So, for the time being at least, everything is going well here – and I have every reason to believe that things will improve still more during the course of the year.

In the second week of August 1989, George received the long-awaited and welcome news that the Kora National Reserve, the land he had doggedly defended for nineteen years, was at last to be made a national park. The old man was overjoyed. Now, it was hoped, Kora, the lions and all the area's wildlife were to be offered greater protection.

Just days later, George Adamson was gunned to death by bandits.

Staying at Kampi ya Simba at this time was a regular German visitor, Inge Ledertheil. Inge was witness to the full horror of the tragedy.

The night before George's death, his wild pride of Growe, One Eye and the sets of youngsters mysteriously appeared at Kampi ya Simba. These wild-born lions, descended from George's rehabilitated lions, like the parents and grandparents, retained a unique bond with George, visiting him from time to time. George had recently been concerned about the pride, having not seen them for many weeks.

That night, watched by Inge and the staff, George, in a time-honoured ritual of Kampi ya Simba, stepped out of the fenced camp and moved amongst his pride, handing them chunks of meat, tokens of his great affection for his lions. When the pride later roared in the darkness, George must have felt a deep and personal contentment.

At noon the following day, a plane flew low over the camp, signalling that it was about to land. Inge and the driver, Bitacha, drove out on the road towards the airstrip to meet the plane and its occupants. Suddenly, shots were heard, bandits appeared from the bush forcing Bitacha to stop the vehicle. Mercilessly, the bandits, demanding money, broke both of Bitacha's legs with an iron bar and began to beat Inge.

George either heard the shots or was warned of the sound of bullets by one of the trackers at camp. He called some staff members, picked up his rifle and handgun and drove hurriedly towards the airstrip. Upon seeing the vehicle and the bandits; he slowed, assessing the situation before roaring forward.

In the ultimate gesture to protect life, George died. He was shot from the side as he reached the bandits and was shot from the back as the vehicle came to a standstill. With him died two of his loyal staff.

The great tragedy was to shock legions of George's friends and supporters worldwide. His murder also had an effect on the three cubs, now a year old, and on Growe and the pride.

In a letter to me, Inge wrote the following:

Sunday afternoon (that day will haunt me for the rest of my life) Rafiki ran away [from the camp] because of all the shooting and spent her very first night alone in the bush. At the time when the rangers were taking the dead and myself back to camp, Growe and her family (all fifteen lions) appeared at camp. I think that is the reason why Rafiki was too scared to come back to camp. [In the past, Growe's pride had shown aggression towards the three cubs.]

Inge was hastily flown out of Kora by military helicopter with George's body beside her. A massive search for the killers took place by seven hundred troops. Within days one of the alleged bandits was arrested at Mbala Mbala, a village twenty miles from Kora.

Nearly one hundred soldiers packed into Kampi ya Simba, and the three cubs were restricted to their enclosure, pacing and calling as George's hornbills, squirrels and guinea fowl (his 'camp family') patiently waited to be fed by George – a nineteen-year-old ritual which had now ceased.

Two and a half months later I was walking with three tumbling, happy young lions – Batian and his sisters – in the African bush. I was not at Kora but hundreds of miles to the south in the Botswana Tuli bushlands – freedom for the three had not died with George.

I gained authorisation from many parties, including both the Kenyan and Botswana governments, to give George's three young lions a home in a privately owned portion of the Tuli bushlands lying at the junction of three countries – Zimbabwe, South Africa and Botswana. The only other option for the cubs, it seemed, was a lifetime in captivity. At Kora, for the foreseeable future, there was no hope of continuing the lions' rehabilitation or contributing to George's wishes for Kora. At least by taking the lions to Botswana, I could attempt to offer freedom to his three much-loved orphans.

Over the next two and a half years, the lions' return to the wild was achieved and freedom found. It was a time of great happiness but also of heartbreak, a time of laughter and a time of tears.

CHAPTER

1

To Be Free

The mighty engines of the Kenya Airways airbus roared as the plane hurtled along the runway of Jomo Kenyatta Airport. As the plane lifted skyward, I gave a sigh of relief. We, the lions and I, were at last on our way to Botswana. To move three young lions from one isolated game reserve in Kenya, seven thousand kilometres south to another isolated game reserve in Botswana, had proved not to be the simplest of undertakings.

Apart from obtaining all the necessary permits, I had, during my time in Nairobi, gained sponsorship to transport the lions to Botswana. The Elsa Trust kindly covered the cost of the Kora/Nairobi leg, and Air Botswana with Kenya Airways (the latter appropriately known as 'The Pride of Africa') sponsored the lions' and my journey to Botswana.

That morning, take-off of flight KQ440 from Nairobi to Harare to Gaborone was delayed due to the loading of three unusual passengers – my lions in three sturdy wooden crates. It seemed at one point that there was not enough room in the hold for all three crates and I was on edge as I stood on the tarmac. Amidst the confusion, a driver of a fork-lift truck had accidentally bumped into one of the crates, Batian's, nearly upturning it. Lions growled, people shouted instructions, others laughed while discussing what was being loaded into the luggage hold of the huge plane.

I darted around checking the lions, talking to officials and then, towards the end of the loading, helplessly watched the proceedings.

I was concerned about the positioning of one of the lion crates – it was slightly tilted in the hold amongst the numerous suitcases and boxes. A Kenya Airways official approached me.

'Look, it's all OK,' he said kindly. Then, sterner, he continued, 'You must board the plane now. Take-off cannot be delayed any longer.'

After one last look at the lions' crates in the hold, and once again thanking various management personnel of the airways, I ran up the steps and, once inside the plane, was guided to my seat.

Just after take-off, I felt a tap on my shoulder. Across the aisle from me was a dark-haired, middle-aged woman wearing khaki safari clothing.

'What was the hold-up?' she enquired in an American, Southern states accent.

'There were problems loading my lions on to the plane,' I replied simply.

'Lions!' she exclaimed loudly, and some heads turned. 'Why didn't someone tell us about this? You surely can't have lions on a plane with people. It must be against international regulations.'

The no-smoking light went off and I hastily lit a cigarette and said in hushed tones, 'It's OK. They're not up here with us, of course. They're in crates in the luggage hold below.'

'What if they get out?' she huffed before turning away.

I had no answer for her – at least, none she'd like to hear – so I sat back thinking, 'Well, this wouldn't have happened in America, I suppose.'

En route to Gaborone, Botswana's capital, the plane was to stop off at Harare in Zimbabwe. When, after landing, as the plane came to a standstill, I asked the hostess if I could inspect the lions before we took off again, she replied that she thought it would be all right.

I went eagerly down the steps on to the tarmac and walked under the belly of the plane to where handlers were pulling Harare-bound luggage from the hold. I spoke to one of the men, explaining that inside the three crates were lions and I wished to check on them. He shook his head as if he hadn't heard correctly.

'Shumba! Shumba!' ('lion' in Sindebele) I said to emphasise what I meant.

The offloading stopped abruptly and I was invited to check on the crates by myself to see if they were still secure. I clambered into the hold and looked in turn into the three crates. The young lions lay still, appearing calm or resigned to their circumstances, and stared with unblinking amber eyes. I called gently to them, thinking how glad I would be when this journey was over. I turned back and assured the handlers that the crates were intact and secure. I then helped pass to the now smiling men the Harare-bound luggage that had been stacked all around the lions' crates.

As the plane finally landed at Gaborone, I was pleased and relieved to see friends and familiar faces waiting on the tarmac to meet me, among them Julie Davidson, my girlfriend, who had a broad, happy smile on her face. She was as relieved as I that the lions and I had arrived. Over the past two and a half weeks, I had phoned her frequently in Botswana to explain the various problems, set-backs and changes of departure dates that had cropped up. At one point, Julie thought we would never make it to Botswana.

Before embarking upon the five-hundred-and-fifty-kilometre truck journey to the North-east Tuli bushlands, the lions rested for a day and a half on a small private game reserve outside Gaborone. They were housed in a large, fenced-off enclosure. Batian, Furaha and Rafiki fed hungrily on the meat provided by the game-reserve owner, Jimmy Kannemeyer, and spent much of their time sprawled in the shade of some bushes. They had survived the flight well. Now only the road journey was to be completed and then it would be over – they would once again be in the wilds.

The following evening, for the third and final time during the journey, the lions were loaded into the crates. A gang of Jimmy's men lifted the crates on to a heavy-duty truck. We were to drive through the night to escape the heat of Botswana's early summer.

As Julie and I were about to leave, it was discovered that the truck's clutch was faulty. A mechanic friend of mine, Alan Jordaan, tinkered with spanners and time ticked by as I fidgeted. Finally, a head emerged from beneath the vehicle and, with hands covered in grease, Alan said, 'Should be OK now, Gareth.'

His words relieved me to an extent, but I still held fears of breaking down in the night with the lions, miles from our destination.

We set off northwards, first through the city. The driver of the truck was named Sonny. We had been assured by his employer at Van & Truck Hire that he was well rested and would be able to drive through the night.

Surprisingly, considering our cargo, we passed through veterinary and police roadblocks on the lonely road without any problems. The news of the lions' arrival in Botswana had been broadcast several times over the local radio station that day. Whenever we were asked what we were transporting, the police or veterinary personnel would inevitably reply to our somewhat unusual answer with, 'Yes, we heard about it on the radio news. Please pass on' – or something similar.

Three hours out of Gaborone, at about one o'clock, a problem arose. I turned to look at Sonny in the gloom of the truck's cab and, to my alarm, noticed his eyes closing momentarily as he drove. I offered to drive and he gratefully accepted. Julie was worried but said little. She knew how exhausted I was, but she also knew how imperative it was to complete the bulk of the journey before the sun rose.

Fortunately, the road was deserted and I gradually got used to the heavy vehicle, its gears and brakes, while Sonny in the cab and the three lions in the back slept. Julie, sitting between Sonny and me, was now very alert, almost constantly staring at me as I drove, making sure that I too did not doze off. Later, Sonny and I took turns with the driving but eventually, an hour before sunrise, we pulled to one side so that everyone could sleep for a short while. Julie and Sonny slept in the cab as I curled up next to the crates in the open back of the vehicle after first checking on the lions.

It was some sixteen hours after leaving Gaborone that we finally arrived at a fenced camp in the North-east Tuli Block – a simple camp which we were later to name Tawana (Little Lion) Camp, and which our initial sponsor, Tuli Safari Lodge, had built for the project.

The journey was over. With the aid of waiting spectators and staff at the camp, I unloaded the three crates into a fenced-off 'cub enclosure'. While a news crew filmed and cameras clicked, I released Batian, Furaha and Rafiki from their crates.

Furaha, with what I was to increasingly understand as her independent character, stepped out, eyes glinting, without any fear. In contrast, Rafiki emerged from her crate with caution – again a reflection of personality – her head low, eyes watchful and in need of the reassurance which I gave to her. Poor Batian was still suffering from the effects of the tranquillising drug and, I feel, motion sickness. As I released him from his crate, he ventured out as gamely as possible, but his co-ordination was awkward and my heart went out to him. I spoke to the three in gentle, soothing tones and encouraged them to drink from the water-bowls which I offered to each of them.

A news crew, who had been brought to the camp by our sponsor, captured these scenes and later, after I had given the lions some meat, I was interviewed in front of the camera. During and after the interview, as people asked further questions, I felt much like Batian, my senses dulled by long travelling and anxiety merged with relief.

The well-wishers, news people and staff departed an hour or so later, leaving the lions, Julie and me alone in the quietness of our new home. In the stillness I suddenly felt such tremendous exhaustion that it was almost painful.

That night, I pulled a stretcher next to the lions' enclosure so that I could be with them. The three lay contentedly together, each one touching the other with either paw, leg or tail, an arm's length from where I lay.

Tiredness, coupled with emotion, welled up in me. I could have wept with relief that the long journey for the lions was over and a new future lay ahead. It had been a strained time. George's death and the nature of it were still very much in my mind as was his ultimate wish for these three young lions – his wish for them 'to be free'.

How does one rehabilitate lions? I had never undertaken such work over an extended period before, with my practical experience being limited to what I had learned from George with the cubs at Kora. The procedures of the rehabilitation of large carnivores have not been written up formally,* primarily because few people have embarked upon such work. It is a great pity that zoologists did not formulate George's findings and understanding of the process of lion rehabilitation into a single journal or paper. I had very few rehabilitation guidelines to go by, apart from the very general information I had gleaned from George and Joy's books.

* The author is currently co-authoring a paper on the rehabilitation and the physical and behavioural development of lions.

I therefore set myself three main rehabilitation guidelines:

1. To familiarise the lions with their new surroundings, thus giving them security and the opportunity of becoming territorial.
2. To give the lions every opportunity to hunt prey, presenting situations to them so that they could begin to polish their inherent knowledge of hunting.
3. To nurture a mutual and deep trust between the lions and myself but, at the same time, ensuring that the lions became increasingly less familiar with people. I hoped that in time they would view man in the same manner as wild lions do.

During the first six months, I would wake before sunrise and prepare to spend most of the day in the wilds with the lions. The lions would begin cooing at me from their enclosure as I quickly dressed, drank a cup of tea, collected my rifle, water-bottle, notepad and camera. I would then walk around to the gate in the cubs' enclosure and open it. All three would bound out, excitedly moaning greetings, rubbing their bodies against me, with Batian normally stopping to rub his tawny head against mine.

The lions would be filled with a sense of fun and excitement which was infectious. With three young lions – now fifteen months old and each weighing sixty to seventy kilograms – tripping over me and dashing around ambushing each other, I would wave goodbye to Julie. Each morning, she would watch the proceedings from behind the camp's twelve-foot fence.

Julie would often not see me again for another eight or even twelve hours until I returned in the evenings as tired, thirsty and hungry as the three cubs. Early every morning the lions and I would set out to hunt and explore, never knowing what situations might arise. Would they make a small kill? Would we encounter elephants? Would Batian again nearly step on a venomous horned adder?

I did not teach the lions how to hunt, they were born with this knowledge, but I would, when sighting antelope, lead them in the direction of the herds. The lions quickly learned that when I began crouching after spotting prey, something lay ahead. They would then move cautiously until they too saw what I was looking at.

As the weeks passed, it was generally they who indicated to me, with head-low stares, that prey had been spotted and a hunt was about to begin. On one occasion, however, I confess that I had to take Batian's unattentive young head between my hands and literally steer his eyes to where a nearby impala stood feeding. Only then did he move into hunting mode.

The cubs' first two kills were examples of how I would attempt to assist the lions with hunting and the reader might be struck by the fact that I was seemingly cruel on such occasions. What must be remembered is that in the wilds, a lioness will deliberately catch a young antelope, for example, and then present it to her cubs. They will then play with it while it is still alive, like a cat with a mouse, before eventually killing it. This happens for a reason, and for the same reason I would, on occasions, present situations to my cubs – so that they could learn from the experience. It would be this acquired knowledge that they would have to depend upon when having to fend for themselves in the future.

The lions' first kill was a genet cat, a spotted, fox-faced little animal the size of a domestic cat which belongs to the mongoose family. One evening, during those early days, as I was returning with the lions to camp, I spied a gold and black tail protruding from a hole in an old log. As I approached the log, the tail slowly disappeared inside, this movement catching Rafiki's attention. As Rafiki sniffed and pawed at the hole and as Batian and Furaha approached curiously, I rattled a stick on the log. Suddenly a little form appeared from the log and dashed away. The hunt was on. The lions bounded after the genet with me following.

The genet was, to my surprise, not caught by one of the more agile females, but by Batian. He did not kill it immediately, but held it close to his head, pinned down by his already hefty paws. He then keenly peered at the protesting genet. I will never forget his expression of surprise and, perhaps, indignation, as suddenly the genet lunged forward and bit him on the nose. Then, repeatedly, the courageous genet pecked at Batian's face with tiny, razor-sharp teeth. Rafiki and Furaha approached and, after growling at them, warning them away from his catch, Batian swiftly bit the genet through its lower body. It died quickly.

Later, after Batian had played with the body, both the lionesses in turn inspected the genet, grimacing after sniffing and mouthing the little form. I watched, feeling a mixture of admiration and sadness for the genet, so courageous against its impossibly large foe. It was a feeling I was to experience many times on similar occasions over the months ahead. If I had not rattled the stick, perhaps the genet would not have bolted out of its safe haven. Coupled with this emotion, though, I was proud of Batian, and when the lions and I returned to camp, I couldn't tell Julie quickly enough of Batian's accomplishment. Such incidents evoked a strange mixture of conflicting emotions within me.

The lions' second kill was also partially influenced by my actions. A few days after the genet incident, I was leading the lions in the direction of a herd of impala which was feeding near a baboon troop. I know, however, that no matter how stealthy our stalk was, it would be impossible to get close to the impala; the keen-eyed baboons would typically give our presence away with loud barks and insults.

As we approached, the inevitable shouts and barks broke out – the impala were alerted, spotted us and the herd rushed away. The baboons then, somewhat surprisingly, moved away down a valley in no real hurry. The lions' hunting blood was up though, excited by the noisy apes. They took off after the baboons in a rush, abandoning for the moment any subtle stalking techniques.

As I was running to catch up with the lions, I suddenly heard ahead of me in the near distance the loud growling of one of the lions and the screams of a baboon. A few minutes later, I found Rafiki standing at the base of a tree staring upwards. In the branches was a large, adult female baboon. She had been injured by Rafiki and moved sluggishly above.

On my arrival, Rafiki turned and moved towards me. As I stroked her head, I heard and then saw the baboon coming down the tree, attempting to flee. As it touched the ground, Rafiki bounded after it. I then lost sight of them both in the scrubby bush, although I heard more growls and screams. I again ran to where the sounds were coming from and saw the baboon, clearly in great pain, slowly moving towards other trees as Rafiki circled it. The baboon, I noticed, had been bitten in the hindquarters and stomach.

Astonishingly, despite its wounds, with courage similar to that displayed by the genet, the baboon turned and attempted to rush at Rafiki with its vicious teeth bared. Rafiki effortlessly skipped away. The baboon then noticed my presence and turned to repeat its display at me. I too moved away, though admittedly not with the grace of Rafiki. The wounded and angry baboon was a terrifying sight and I knew what formidable weapons their teeth were; baboons have been known to disembowel attacking dogs.

The baboon then slowly limped to a tree and, after pulling itself up, slumped in the branches. Rafiki repeatedly climbed upwards, intimidating further the weakening baboon. Later, as Rafiki began to lose interest in the baboon, I shot it, justifying my action as it was dying a slow, painful death while its carcass would represent to the lions the culmination of a successful hunt.

As the baboon fell to the ground, Rafiki leapt forward, grasping it instinctively at the base of the spine, inflicting her own *coup de grâce*. At this point, Batian and Furaha reappeared, trotting forward and panting, obviously returning from their chase after the rest of the troupe. Noticing the other two, Rafiki dragged the baboon into some thick bushes, her mouth clamped around its neck. Her muffled growls clearly indicated her possession of the kill to her brother and sister. She then instinctively began to pluck at the baboon's long fur for almost forty-five minutes before beginning to feed. I sat and watched and later saw Rafiki suddenly leave the carcass, allowing Batian to take possession.

Baboons are by no means a preferred form of prey for lions. However, as similar situations arose, I began to realise that the young lions would take every opportunity to attack baboon, which became what I can only describe as 'practice prey'. On some occasions, the carcasses were barely eaten.

This baboon incident reminded me of an earlier time when, in the Tuli, I observed three lionesses deliberately instigating an attack on a baboon troupe for the benefit of their large cubs. Again, the lionesses initiated the attack solely for the purpose of teaching their offspring. After encircling then rushing at the troupe, the lionesses moved away to some shade, allowing the cubs to dash forward and take over.

On that occasion, four young baboons were killed by the cubs who were, in turn, partially intimidated by the return of some large adult baboons. The adults taunted the cubs, luring them away from low trees containing a multitude of females and infants. As the cubs moved away, the formerly entrapped baboons leapt from the bushes and trees, escaping into the undergrowth.

Another creature frequently pursued by my lions in those early weeks was the monitor lizard. Two kinds of these large lizards occur in the reserve – the water-loving Nile monitor and the stout rock monitor, which the cubs would most commonly come across. Full-grown, they are some one and a half metres long and are well known for their whipping tail if approached. These creatures were attacked by the lions merely as practice prey as I never saw them attempting to eat the lizards.

One evening, the lions came across a monitor which rushed across the ground in front of them and then climbed into a short tree. Furaha leapt into the air and swiped the monitor off a branch. Rafiki pounced on it as it fell and quickly nipped it in the lower spine. All three lions played with it before, astonishingly, the monitor avenged itself somewhat. Rafiki took the lizard's head into her mouth whereupon she was promptly bitten on the tongue and there the monitor clung determinedly. She pulled at the monitor's body, but in turn was inflicting pain upon herself as the monitor held on with a vice-like grip. I watched and chuckled as Rafiki pushed her tongue out with the dangling monitor attached, then pulled her tongue back in with a third of the monitor also disappearing into her mouth.

She became terribly frustrated, growling loudly, but because of the monitor's position, her growl sounded unlike any I had ever heard. Furaha and Batian were startled by the growls and looked around them, thinking that other lions were nearby. Batian even ran off a little way. It took another five minutes before Rafiki managed to release the monitor from her bleeding tongue. She instantly moved away, leaving the lizard on the ground, and walked towards Furaha at the water-hole. For some reason, Batian returned to the lizard and carried it off to the water-point. He dropped the lizard, drank and then left it where it had fallen.

On another occasion, a monitor got the better of all three lions. When this particular lizard was encircled by the lions, it put up an extraordinary threat display. The lions attempted to grasp the lizard with their paws but were greatly disturbed by its lashing tail and by behaviour I had never witnessed before in a monitor lizard. The metre-long lizard began to leap forwards and upwards with its mouth agape, bumping against the lions' heads and legs. The lizard's behaviour so frustrated the lions that short fights broke out amongst them. Whenever the lions bumped into my foot or the rifle butt, they would leap away, fearing it was the lizard. This confrontation went on for some twenty minutes until a passing zebra herd distracted the lions and the lizard was left in peace.

One other rather unusual creature which the young lions would hunt was tortoise. On many occasions while with the lions, I would see one of them stop and sink its head low – the stalking position. I would naturally then look keenly ahead, trying to see what was being hunted. The lion would invariably creep forward, then dash ahead and pounce on to a spot on the ground. Another tortoise, I would realise.

The tortoise's hard shell would be gnawed at and very occasionally bitten through. Sometimes, the lions would play with the tortoise, whose head would be tucked tightly inside the shell, then leave it upside down as they became distracted or disinterested. It was not uncommon for me to have to turn the tortoises the right way up as the lions walked away. Many escaped completely unscathed, apart from a few more scratches on their hard shells.

Walking away, I would imagine the tortoise's perspective on the incident. With its head just an inch or two above the stony ground, it would trundle along to only it knew where. Suddenly a huge shadow would be cast over it and, as the tortoise hastily drew in its head and legs, it would feel a tremendous bump. Hidden within its shell, it would be cuffed by paws, unceremoniously dragged along the ground and left upside down. Minutes later, inexplicably to the tortoise, it would be righted once again and find itself alone. It would cautiously emerge its head, then its legs, and peer around, before trundling along once again. As they are long-living animals, such incidents are probably not uncommon to them. To humanise the situation, one can visualise the ancient old tortoise mumbling like a most put-upon grandfather grumbling about noisy children, 'Blasted lion cubs again,' before continuing on its way.

Those early days in the Tuli with the lions were a time of great learning, not only for Batian, Furaha and Rafiki, but also for me. In my privileged situation with the young pride in the wilds, I witnessed unique interactions between the lions and their prey. I also learned about many aspects of lion behaviour and indeed the manner in which I had to interrelate with the lions.

During the heat of the day, the lions and I would rest, sprawled in whatever shade was available. I would occupy some of these hottest hours by writing up notes on my observations of the lions' return to the wild. Once, when working on my notes while lying with the lions out of the sun, a somewhat amusing incident with an elephant took place . . .

We – the lions and I – were resting in the shade of a large tree. Nearby was a water-hole which had recently been replenished with rain and was filled with clear waters. As I turned over a page from a collection of loose notes, I noticed Furaha next to me slowly roll on to her back with that lazy indulgence that only lions seem to enjoy. With her legs pointing upwards, she exposed her white underparts. However, her relaxed state changed abruptly as her head lolled towards the direction of the water-hole. Suddenly, in a flurry, she hastily righted herself and stood up, staring ahead. Her movements alerted both Batian and Rafiki, who awoke with a start.

There at the water-hole less than fourteen metres away, a young adult bull elephant stood motionless. It seems incredible that the elephant was so close and yet I had heard nothing of its approach. Elephants are well known for their ability to move through the African bush quite silently – termed as grey ghosts by some bush dwellers.

I felt tiny sitting under the tree, staring up at the bull. My reaction was instantaneous, instinctive and motivated by self-preservation; I fled. My papers dropped from my hands, were caught by a gusting breeze and flew into the air like giant confetti. As I reached the bank of a small streambed, I stopped to look back. Batian had dashed away with me and stood nearby, staring at the elephant. Rafiki was between him and Furaha, who stood unmoving where just seconds before we had all been resting peacefully.

I groaned inwardly as I saw Furaha begin to move into a stalking stance. Surely this young lioness was not about to take on four tons of elephant. I imagined her, largely inexperienced in the ways of elephant, being slammed against a tree by one tremendous sweep of the bull's trunk. Rafiki too began to copy her sister while, like me, Batian hung back observing. Both he and I were watchful, and neither of us as enthusiastically fuelled with the spirit of a somewhat daunting hunt as the lionesses.

I was helpless to intervene. The lionesses slowly crept forward, hiding behind logs and bushes. The bull was, however, now very aware of our presence, twisting his trunk into the air, attempting to catch our scent. The two sisters crept ever closer and suddenly the unexpected occurred. The elephant let out a loud, high-pitched trumpet, turned and crashed away. His hindquarters, as he ran, reminded me of someone wearing baggy and wrinkled old trousers ten sizes too big.

Furaha and Rafiki bounded after the bull. I came out of the shadows and watched with amusement as Batian hastily attempted to catch up with his sisters, enthusiastically joining in the chase now that the elephant was fleeing.

I stood alone and listened as the sounds of the elephant charging through the bush became increasingly distant. While I awaited the lions' return, I walked around searching for my scattered notes. Eventually, three panting lions reappeared. They drank thirstily from the water-hole and then greeted me happily. They had obviously thoroughly enjoyed seeing off the elephant. Before we headed back to camp, the lions rested while I searched fruitlessly for one still missing page, which I never found.

Our arrival at camp that evening was typical of many evenings during the first few months in the Tuli. I opened the gate to let the lions into their enclosure, as always having to wait for Batian as he plodded along behind. I would call to Julie, who was normally busy in the kitchen area of camp. Then, as the lions drank from the water-bowls, Julie and I would begin to talk about the day's happenings before feeding the three.

Meat would have been taken out of an old gas freezer by our only staff member, an elderly Tswana man named John Knox. John was a roguish but very likeable character who did not stay with us long. His tenure at Tawana Camp was shortened due to his extremely large and overbearing wife. One day she appeared in the reserve after a long absence in South Africa. Upon meeting John, she attacked him with scandalous accusations, claiming that she had heard that in her absence he had had a bevy of girlfriends with him at our camp. This was, of course, quite untrue, but, at his wife's insistence, he left our employ. We were sorry to see him go as we liked old John. So too, it seemed, did the lions, particularly in the evenings when he approached their enclosure carrying buckets full of meat. The lions were at that time still familiar with people. However, I feel that as this familiarity faded over the months, they would have retained a friendship with John if he had stayed with us.

During those evenings, it became clear to me that I had to be very aware of not standing or sitting close to Julie in front of the lions. Upon seeing me with Julie, they would become agitated and pace up and down in their enclosure. They were clearly possessive of me. When this occurred, I would leave Julie and spend time with the lions, calming them. Strangely, as I settled the lions, any one of them, but particularly Rafiki, would grip on to the skin of my arm with their teeth, holding me firmly. They rarely bit too hard and never broke the skin. This was a clear demonstration of their possessiveness and strong emotional attachment to me.

When John was with us, he seemed very proud of his role with 'Ra di Tau' – the Lion Man, as I was nicknamed by the local Tswana people. It also appeared that on John's day off, the stories he told of his work (heavily embellished and exaggerated by the consumption of alcoholic beverages) reached epic proportions. After John had been away, people working at other camps in the reserve would question us as to whether it was true that John walked, without fear, amongst the lions, instructing them to hunt impala for him like a pack of dogs!

However, just before John was taken away by his wife, an incident took place which illustrated to us that John was not as comfortable in his work, nor as completely happy about his safety in our camp, as we had thought. Late one afternoon, John and I were working together at camp while Julie was away for the night. I had left the lions in the bush earlier in the day to let them return on their own in the evening. As John and I were putting the rather rough finishing touches to a small so-called 'office' constructed from wood offcuts, we heard the lions cooing outside camp. I went through the gate to greet them as John watched from inside.

As I bent down to head rub with Furaha, with Rafiki next to me (and without first checking where Batian was), I suddenly felt a heavy weight crash into me. I fell backwards and went sprawling, ending up three or four metres from where I had been standing. Batian, unseen by me, had joyously flung his now considerable eighty-odd kilograms up on to me.

I remember thinking as I landed on the dirt that it was imperative that I get up quickly, for all the lions could bundle on to me. My fears disappeared as I looked up. Rafiki was head-rubbing with Furaha while, in front of them, Batian approached me, looking amiable and calm. I stood up using Batian's shoulder as leverage.

My thoughts turned to John and I looked into the camp and saw him standing with a terrified expression on his face.

After dusting the soil from my back and allowing my heart time to resume its normal rhythm, I stepped back into camp through the gate. I walked up to John, assuring him that I was all right and that Batian had not attacked me but had been over-enthusiastic in his greeting.

John looked worse than I felt. He then said, 'I was so worried. I thought now you are dead, finished. The lion had knocked you dead.' I was touched by his apparent concern and repeated that all was fine.

John spoke again in a tone indicating that I had not understood him properly. 'No, no. I was worried because if you were dead, I would be alone in this camp tonight. I wouldn't even be able to go away. Julie is only coming back tomorrow.'

I laughed as he did, both of us laughing for different reasons. John's concern was pragmatic, but his attitude towards what he thought had occurred did have some point. To him, if I was dead, I was dead, and nothing was going to change that. But he would be very much alive and totally alone.

Being knocked to the ground by Batian, though, was the only time with the lions that I felt I was in a potentially dangerous situation. My answer when questioned by people about my safety with the lions is normally, 'If I did get hurt, it would almost certainly be due to my own wrong actions or body language.'

This incident was an example. Instead of immediately greeting the lioness, I should have checked on Batian's whereabouts first. Early on in their rehabilitation, the lions had to be broken of the habit of jumping up on to me. By shouting or tapping them with a stick, they soon stopped this habit, although Rafiki occasionally still does it to this day. It is always when either she or I have been away for an extended period or if she is disturbed in some way and in need of emotional security.

CHAPTER

2

The Tuli – Salmon's Story

How can you buy or sell the sky and the warmth of
the land? . . . if we do not own the freshness of the
breeze and the reflections of the water, how can you
buy them?

> Words of Chief Seathl to
> the Americans who wanted to
> buy the land from the Indians

The Tuli bushlands, the lions' new home, is not a national park,
but an area of some one thousand, two hundred square kilometres
encompassing adjoining portions of Botswana and Zimbabwe. The
Botswana portion is an area of private reserves owned by predominantly absentee white South Africans. The Zimbabwe portion is
known as the Tuli Safari Area, a controlled hunting area, owned by
the state and run by that country's wildlife department. Fortunately
no fences split or divide these areas. Thus wildlife has free movement
within the total area.

The Tuli bushlands is a harsh but beautiful remnant of wilderness
which, unlike that land beyond its boundaries, was not lost to man's
progress, technology and civilisation. When describing the Tuli, its
surrounding areas, its history and the pressures that face it, I often
think back to a conversation I once had with an elderly black man
who was born in the vicinity of the Tuli's southern boundary, the

Limpopo river. The old man's name is Salmon Maomo. He is South African and today acts as a foreman on an empty South African border farm on the Limpopo's banks. Through his now rheumy eyes, he has witnessed the passing of this century and the enormous changes that have taken place in this portion of Africa. He saw what was lost and what survived.

My conversation with old Salmon took place beneath a great Mashatu tree on the banks of the waterless Limpopo river. Why the river is dry is part of the story of the Tuli area, and this is where I shall start.

I asked Salmon that day to describe to me how the Limpopo was when he was a young man. He replied sternly, as if angered, saying only two words at first, 'It flowed.'

Today, sadly, this stretch of one of Africa's legendary rivers never flows as it once did. The river's waters exist, but lie unseen beneath the sands for much of the year. With the coming of the summer rains (if sufficient rain falls), the Limpopo rises forcefully, flowing quickly with silty waters, but soon slows and then dries.

The water table of the Limpopo has lowered alarmingly in the past twenty years. Further upstream, dams hold the waters, while, on the South African farms, engines and pumps above the bore-holes have sucked up the waters from the ground for agricultural purposes. The river is dying and with it sections of riverine bush along its banks – the trees literally dying of thirst.

If a soaring eagle had been flying above where old Salmon and I were talking, it would have looked down to a contrasting view on either side of the dry river. On the Tuli side lies wild bushlands, the river banks fringed by dark-green canopies of the riverine trees (and patches of grey where the trees have died). The riverine tapers inland to areas of spindly acacia trees which lead on to open plains. As the ancient Limpopo valley rises, the eagle would have seen dry streams, fanned like fingers heading southwards to the Limpopo and, at their source, during the rains, the catchment area in the north. If it was autumn, the land would be one of russet colours, red soil, red elephants, orange leaves upon trees such as the mopane and the commiphora, the red bush willow.

On the southern side of the Limpopo, the eagle would have viewed a different land. Along the border between South Africa and Botswana, the great swathes of bushlands, like those of the

Tuli, have disappeared. Instead now there are wide green sheets of farming areas, fences and farm-labourers' compounds. A straight tar road runs northwards to the border and another joins it, cutting east to west.

The land further south is divided by the game fences of the game farms. These are comparatively small areas of land set aside for the 'utilisation' of the wild animals which each farm holds. From April onwards, it is an area where shots are frequently heard, popping here, there and everywhere when the hunting season begins. Here, the wildlife cannot move as it historically did, it is now restricted to ecologically (though not necessarily, in the short term, economically) unviable areas of land used by the hunters from the cities who annually sate their bloodlust. Game animals are bought and sold like livestock in the South African game industry. Antelope with wide eyes are loaded into trucks and driven to these farms. The animals are unloaded, seemingly free again, but find themselves restricted by the fences – these farms are a sad facsimile of the wilds as they once were.

In the corner of our eagle's eyes, like a grey battleship amidst motionless waves of the blue horizon, would have appeared a large diamond mine in the south. In a vast area around the mine, the De Beers company has bought up many game farms and, to its credit, has brought down the dividing fences and is developing a large game reserve called Venetia. A worrying aspect of the presence of this mine, though, is the operation's demands upon local water resources, a factor which could be impacting further on the drastically declined water table of the Limpopo valley to which the ecology of the Tuli bushlands and surrounding areas is inextricably linked.

'There were crocodiles too,' the old man continued, 'large ones . . . and hippos . . . our women had to be careful when drawing water.'

'And lions?' I asked, pointing into the northern Transvaal, south of the Limpopo's banks.

'Yes, they were here. Many in my father's time. And you know where that mine is now? Well, that was a place where many lions lived.'

I asked Salmon the inevitable question, though I knew what his answer would be.

'What happened to the lions, Salmon? There are none now. Only those which come from our side in the Tuli and are shot by the farmers.'

He replied that they had all gone. Like the river, the lions of the northern Transvaal are gone. Salmon told me how, for a time, lions were frequently killed by the white men. With less lions, the shootings became less frequent and today much excitement occurs amongst the farmers and hunters when a Tuli lion inadvertently crosses (or is lured across) the dry Limpopo into South Africa . . . and inevitably, like its ancestors, the lion is always destroyed. Early cattle ranching by the whites, coupled with their lust for hunting, ensured that in yet another portion of southern Africa, the lion is locally extinct.

'When the lions were finished here, some still lived over there,' said Salmon, pointing north to the Tuli.

The lions of the Tuli, though, were caught up in a conflict with man, acting to protect his livestock. In the Tuli between the 1880s and the early 1960s, periodic attempts at cattle ranching were made. During the 1950s alone, a hundred and fifty lions were destroyed in the Tuli.

I remember hearing one story of the slaying of lions at that time. Some cattle ranchers hunted down a group of lionesses – all were shot and one was found to be heavily in milk. Unceremoniously, the dead lionesses were loaded on to a cart drawn by donkeys and taken to the ranchers' camp. The bodies were skinned before their naked forms were left outside the camp. That night, the rancher heard the cries of small cubs. The little ones were hungry and had, somehow, sensed where their now mutilated mother lay. Although the cubs found her, in turn the rancher found them and soon they too were to lie still and lifeless like their mother. They were shot.

By the mid 1960s, only a tiny, shattered remnant of the Tuli lion population remained. In the north, in the Tuli Safari area, other lions fortuitously existed, and collectively these lions and those in the Tuli represented the sole surviving lions from an area that had once extended throughout the northern Transvaal in South Africa, eastern Botswana and much of south-western Zimbabwe. These lions, probably numbering less than fifty, were the last survivors of the original population of hundreds – a population representing a mere strand of what was once the wide web of lion life existing throughout southern Africa.

Fortunately for the Tuli lions, in January 1964 some Botswana residents of the area applied to the Botswana Wildlife Department for the banning of lion (and leopard) hunting in the Tuli. The Wildlife Department approved the proposal and although lions continued to be shot in the Zimbabwe portion, no lion has since been legally killed in the Botswana portion. Illegal killings continued, however, and still take place today.

The wild lands where I was now rehabilitating the lions traditionally belonged to the Ngwato tribe, whose Paramount Chief in 1880 was Khama. He was a man of great integrity and has been described as one of the greatest chiefs in southern Africa. Sir Seretse Khama, his son, became Botswana's first President in 1966.

Due to Boer aggression and cattle raiding, Khama III sought British protection for his people and land. In time, this was achieved when what was referred to as 'Khama's Country' became the British Bechuanaland Protectorate. This period in Africa's history represents a scramble – a scramble for concessions, colonisation and mining rights.

During this time, a land concession was granted to Cecil John Rhodes's powerful British South Africa Company. The concession included what today is the Tuli. Rhodes secured the land as part of his plan to establish a railway running from the Cape to Cairo. But the costs of bridging the numerous rivers and streams of this region made the route unsuitable and eventually the land was sold as farms. Thus was born the beginnings of what are the Tuli farms today or, collectively, what is termed as the Northern Tuli Game Reserve by the current landowners.

This portion of southern Africa was historically rich in wildlife, but so much was destroyed by white travellers and hunters in the nineteenth century and into the twentieth century. So drastic was the destruction that, by 1870, hunters from the south were moving north through the Tuli and deep into what is now Zimbabwe in search of elephants and their ivory. The southern African elephant herds, including those of the Tuli, were all but completely lost during that time.

Today, however, the Tuli once again has large numbers of

elephant. Due to persecution to the west and east, refugee herds from as far away as Mozambique sought sanctuary in the Tuli and, as I write, the population is in excess of six hundred. Not all the variety of species that were once indigenous to the Tuli still exist here. The black rhino is gone, as are the buffalo, the wild dog, roan antelope, reedbuck, red hartebeest, gemsbok and, to a large degree, Salmon's crocodiles and hippos. No longer does anyone fear venturing down the Limpopo's banks on the Tuli; what is there to fear from sand?

Over the past thirty years, with the more enlightened times, the landowners of the Tuli bushlands have become less hunting-orientated and more conservation-minded. During these years, the remaining animal herds built up and thankfully none of the landowners erected game fences to prevent the free movement of the animals. In neighbouring South Africa, 'ownership' of wildlife is dictated by the land on which the animals live – this has prompted fences to be erected. In Botswana, however, wildlife belongs to the state, not the individual landowner, and thus in the Tuli, landowners had no motivation to fence off their lands. But, conflictingly coupled with this, the continued existence of wild animals on such lands largely depends on the attitude of the landowner. The state's access to this wildlife as a national resource seems limited by present laws pertaining to wildlife on private land generally.

In the 1970s and early 1980s, 'utilisation' of wildlife became a popular concept in conservation in southern Africa – 'utilisation' meaning animals being culled or commercially hunted, with the monies generated from these activities supposedly being channelled back into conservation. The utilisation concept rose its head in the private Tuli reserves in the late 1970s with the landowner of a substantial area approaching the Botswana Wildlife Department with a proposal to establish culling practices on his land. He was turned down, but took the Wildlife Department to court, only to lose the case with costs.

The landowners of the Tuli at that time had become divided on what strategy to adopt for the whole area. The ensuing infighting and strife amongst them led to the matter being debated in Parliament in Botswana. A meeting between the Tuli landowners and the government was arranged after a motion was called by the National Assembly for the government to acquire the Tuli farms for the establishment of a national game reserve.

This motion was a product of the nation's dissatisfaction and concern about the future of wildlife in the Tuli. The lack of co-operation and adoption of a common conservation strategy by the Tuli landowners indicated to the government that the future of this wild land and its animals was very doubtful. This resulted in the government removing the landowners' hunting rights and determining that no culling, etc. would take place without the permission of the Wildlife Department. Additionally, the purchase or sale of lands in the Tuli became subject to ministerial approval and a thirty per cent transfer duty, payable to the government, was imposed on the sale of any of the land.

Today, the Tuli is still privately owned and its owners are relatively more united in their conservation outlook. Giraffe, for example, were reintroduced into the area in the 1980s. But still there exists a great need for the landowners to evolve an active conservation strategy for the entire area. Anti-poaching units to operate throughout the Tuli, for example, desperately need to be established by the landowners.

Now tourism exists in some of the private reserves of the Tuli; luxury lodges have been built and game drives are undertaken by guides in off-road vehicles. Despite the development of tourism, though, at the time of writing there is generally little protection of wildlife occurring – one prays this will, with time and the realisation and implementation of responsibility, change for the better.

More or less at the same time as the lions and I arrived, some private reserves in the east, where much of my lions' lives were to be spent, had been consolidated into a conservancy with a common conservation strategy. This was initiated by a young conservationist, Bruce Petty, who became warden of this area which he named the Charter Reserve. This conservancy concept being developed by Bruce was in its infancy and was inhibited by a lack of funding, but at least the idea had been introduced; a journey, after all, must begin with a single step.

Bruce Petty's conservancy concept desperately needs to be applied to the entire Botswana Tuli bushlands. But unless holistic conservation attitudes evolve in the minds of many of the Tuli landowners, the land will continue to be injured and its wild inhabitants will continue to exist precariously without essential custodianship.

I recall a passage from Kuki Gallmann's book, *I Dreamed of Africa*, which deals with the issue of land ownership.

'Landowner?' I spoke from my heart. So often, I had thought about that very point. 'I do not feel like a landowner. I cannot believe that we really own the land. It was there before us, and it will be there after we pass. I believe we can only take care of it – as trustees, for our lifetime. I was not even born here. It is for me a great privilege to be responsible for a chunk of Africa.'

Many who 'own' wild lands in southern Africa and elsewhere could be inspired by these words of compassion and vision.

The lack of preservation generally in the private reserves is very much part of what makes up the story of our lives with the lions. I strove to enable the lions to live wild lives, fending for themselves, but, at the same time, I had to ensure that they were not endangered by the various threats that affect wildlife in the Tuli, such as poaching, illegal hunting or conflict with livestock. The Tuli and its animals deserve greater protection, having survived the pressures of the past and having the potential of being a wildlife region of international importance.

My deep feelings for the protection of the Tuli originate from my past work in the area between 1983 and 1986. At that time, I was twenty years old and employed as a ranger in one of the largest private reserves. As part of my duties, I was encouraged to undertake an observer's study of the Tuli lion population. What began as a low-key study of a single lion population led me to realise the true plight of the lion as a species throughout Africa. As a young ranger, I entered deeply into the lions' lives and was shocked and saddened to realise what was happening to the Tuli lion population.

Poaching and other factors reduced the Tuli lion prides which I knew by almost fifty per cent in a mere two and a half years. The number of lions in the Tuli bushlands dropped from almost sixty to only twenty-nine. Some of the lions were shot as cattle killers in livestock areas on two of the Tuli's boundaries, and others were illegally and cruelly lured on to the neighbouring South African farms to be shot in 'sport'. Most of the lions lost, though, died in poachers' lethal snares – simple lassoes of wire which choked the lions and so many animals to death. Even elephants did not escape the effects of this form of poaching. I know of a young elephant that somehow still survives, despite having lost its entire trunk in a snare six years ago. I have seen, not uncommonly, other elephants with shortened trunks which have been severed by the wire.

The results of my observations, feelings and actions during that period of my life led to my first book, *Cry for the Lions*, which I wrote in an attempt to draw attention to the problems affecting the Tuli lions and thus to prompt action for their greater protection. Naïvely believing in the power of the pen, I felt sure that this protection would occur.

I left the Tuli to write the book, and after completing it, for the next two years I focused my attention on the lion's continental plight. I travelled thousands of kilometres across southern Africa, met George Adamson for the first time, worked with George and then wrote another book, the themes remaining constant – 'lion, man, encroachment, poaching, guns, bullets, death' – and, some-how, 'hope'.

During this time, my memories of the Tuli and its lions stayed with me. In my heart, I knew that one day I had to return. In the three and a half years I was away from the Tuli, I would hear news of the area: 'Another lion snared . . . It's thought that the Kali sisters' pride has been shot . . . The old pride male, Darky, was caught, but bit his way out of the poacher's cable snare.' From other sources, I also heard, untruthfully, that the lion population was stabilising, in fact increasing, and the unkind untruths gave me false hope. I'd failed to recognise the irony in what was being said.

In 1989, I was about to return to the area and, among other projects such as environmental education, attempt to re-evaluate the Tuli lion population and establish greater protective measures for these lions and all the wildlife of the Tuli bushlands. With George's murder, the rehabilitation of the three lion cubs became my main objective in the area.

Returning to the Tuli bushlands was to me a homecoming and, soon after our arrival, I was prompted to write the following words – words that record my feelings on being back where I truly felt I belonged. I was writing to the bushlands.

> *Back again in the land I had known*
> *Back again where my heart was left*
> *I am here! I am here! A tear touches my lips*
> *At last we are together again*
> *I embrace you, old mother.*

Oh wild world encased in man's grasping hands
Oh wild world clinging to your ancient balance
Your seasons, life and death.
How long have we together – free?
How long have you, and me?

Since I was last embraced by your spirit
You seem shrunken, your vastness diminished
Have you become less or I more?

No matter! We are together again
And I embrace you, old mother.

Life is a cycle, is it not?
As the trees grow, I grew under your eyes
Then
I went away like the eagles north
And seasons passed with no return
For long your breeze spoke the whispers of beckoning
Then I returned at last, and was caressed by your touch.

I could die here, and so be it.
I am here! I am here! A tear touches my lips
At last we are together again and
I embrace you, old mother.

Back under the Mashatu tree with old Salmon, I asked him what he thought of my work; returning lions to the wild and giving protection to wildlife. He thought for a while and then said, 'It's good . . . my grandchildren do not know a lion like I once did or our ancestors did. The children only know lions from pictures.' He paused, nodding his head sadly. 'The white man destroyed so much, like the animals, and like our real culture, and now he is trying to bring the animals back.' Then he faltered and left the subject disparagingly.

I then realised his message. With the animals of the old man's time largely gone in neighbouring South Africa, the land has altered and his culture eroded. He and his people, like the land, have become isolated, the links broken, and perhaps he, in his twilight years, can see no future in the way he once recognised a future as a young man – too much has altered.

In my conversation with the old man, I gained an insight into the passage of time and the changes that had taken place during the

Tuli's history. Salmon's story illustrated that somehow, through that time, that erosion of life, the Tuli has survived, unlike those lands and animals lost in the south.

The essence of the Tuli's history and our shared environment in general always reminds me of the message in the following words written by North American Indian Chief Seathl in a letter to the President of the United States of America dated 1885:

> *What is man without the beast?*
> *If all the beasts were gone,*
> *Man would die from a great loneliness of spirit.*
> *For whatever happens to the beast*
> *Also happens to the man.*
> *All things are connected.*
> *Whatever befalls the earth,*
> *Befalls the sons of the earth.*

At the onset of the lion rehabilitation project, I wished for the sake of the lions, for the Tuli, to embrace the message of those words; to work towards a greater balance between the wilds and man and, in turn, reduce some of the conflict which has existed for so long in this portion of southern Africa.

CHAPTER

3

Life at Tawana

Tawana Camp lies in a beautiful valley system just south of the boundary with the Tuli Safari Area in Zimbabwe. Like George's 'Kampi ya Simba' (Camp of Lions) at Kora, Tawana is surrounded by a twelve-foot fence, literally to keep people in and lions and other animals out. Also like Kampi ya Simba, our camp has been described by some of our infrequent visitors as a 'zoo in reverse', with man behind the fence and the wilds and all its life on the outside.

Bush life was a new experience to Julie, having been brought up in city environs and working previously in an office. However, Julie had within her an empathy for the wilds and quickly adapted to her new surroundings – as the lions did to their new home.

At the beginning of the rehabilitation project, people who knew Julie in South Africa, where she was born, expressed the opinion that she would not last long in the bush and would soon return 'home'. This, I am sure, was because of her apparent 'diminutive' nature, coupled with her slightness of build and air of vulnerability. Her closely knit family also held grave reservations about her moving into the wilds. However, nobody took into consideration Julie's own growing aspirations, needs and hopes. What transpired in time was that Julie proved the doubters wrong and she showed her true resourceful and determined character, qualities which had been previously suppressed.

Prior to the cubs' arrival in Botswana, Julic and I had not lived together as a couple and I held private thoughts as to whether or not our young relationship would quickly falter and fail in the bush. I too, however, underestimated Julie's reserves and patience.

Living and working together in the Botswana bushlands, returning three lions to the wilds, may indeed sound like an exotic and romantic situation for a young couple to find themselves in and, in a sense, it was. But the realities of such a life can create tremendous pressures on two people. Such a life either breaks or strengthens the relationship. In our case, over the next two years, the breaks almost occurred, but the relationship endured – a relationship which grew and matured between two people, due primarily to shared experiences, trials and tribulations, sorrows and triumphs.

While I roamed with my young lions in those early months, Julie would go about her work in the camp. Every morning, she would start by sweeping and tidying the camp, thankless tasks as the early summer winds prior to the rains would whip up dust and leaves and send them billowing back into the little half-walled kitchen and the tents. Mopane flies would buzz and settle on her face and in her eyes as she washed plates or clothes in the large plastic bowl.

The facilities at Tawana were basic, particularly for someone brought up with the comforts of the city. Our toilet was a deep hole in the ground – a 'long drop' – crowned by an upturned lower jawbone of an elephant which acted as the 'seat'. Unfortunately, a large spitting cobra took up residence from time to time beneath the planking upon which the jawbone rested – and this led to some hair-raising encounters between us and the reptile.

Julie, one morning, was about to use the long drop when she suddenly saw the six-foot cobra in upright 'spitting mode' beside the jawbone – understandably, she fled. When I returned with the lions that evening, she informed me of the shock she had received upon seeing the snake and announced that we should not venture into the toilet for a day or so. Chuckling at the situation, I agreed that we should give the cobra time to move off.

However, the following morning, before sunrise, I sleepily ventured to the long drop. I sat upon the jawbone, contemplating the day ahead of me. My musings were interrupted by a rustle below me in the dark hole and my mind clicked and focused. 'The cobra!' I thought and literally catapulted out of the toilet, my heart beating wildly. It was Julie's turn to laugh at me – the cobra, or whatever was moving in that deep pit, had really caught me with my pants down!

Our bathroom was a three-sided wooden structure next to the long drop. A bucket acted as both bath and shower, and here too the cobra would occasionally venture. The camp fence was just two metres from this ablution area and, not unusually, Julie or I might discover that our bathing or other activities were being scrutinised by the three lions, peering in with muzzles pressed against the fence. Sometimes in the evenings while Julie was busy washing in the bathroom, I would hear a rustling nearby in the bush. Then I would hear Julie saying, 'Hello, cubs,' before venturing out with sopping hair and a towel wrapped around her to tell me that the lions had arrived.

Tawana Camp had no tapped water or bore-hole, so all our water had to be brought to camp in an old forty-four-gallon drum on the back of our vehicle. Every three or four days, Julie would drive to the nearest camp, some thirty minutes away, to fill the drum for our drinking, cooking and washing needs.

On such a 'water trip' during the early months, Julie had her first close encounter with an irascible Tuli elephant. She was accompanied that day by a friend of ours visiting from Britain and by old John Knox. Julie drove out of the camp with our friend beside her in the cab and John sitting on the open back of the vehicle next to the drum. Along the way, they came across an elephant herd watering at a rain-filled pan. She stopped to let our friend photograph and watch the herd. Suddenly, there was a tap on the back window. Our friend turned and saw John frantically waving at her. Unfortunately for John, she thought that he was just being friendly, somehow misinterpreting his terrified grimace as a smile. Our friend waved back at John, smiling brightly. Julie then turned and saw John beginning to crouch desperately beneath the back seat. Luckily, from the corner of her eye, she saw a huge grey shape bearing soundlessly down on the vehicle. Instinctively she slammed her foot on the accelerator, not stopping until they reached their destination. Tuli elephants have a reputation for aggression – an understandable aggression when one considers their historical persecution by man.

Later I learned that while the two women were watching the peaceful herd, John, to his horror, had seen a large tuskless cow elephant charging towards the vehicle from some distance. He told me later that if Julie had not moved the vehicle when she did, he had no doubt that they would have been hit.

He had tapped on the window and gestured to warn the women of the situation and had then had our friend smiling and waving at him. Thinking the two women mad, he prepared himself for the elephant's impact by trying to hide under the seat. Although I did not witness the elephant's charge, I tend to agree with old John's belief that the vehicle would have been hit. An elephant charging noiselessly and at speed occurs rarely and indicates that the animal means business, unlike a mock charge which consists of much noise, trumpeting, short rushes forward and the flapping of ears.

Unlike a lot of people, Julie does not need company constantly around her, being content to be on her own for long periods of time. She does, however, have strong maternal feelings and at the onset of the project, longed to rear a baby animal. Bearing this in mind, I would keep an eye open for any abandoned babies. In the months ahead, Julie became foster mother to a porcupine, a clutch of baby weaver birds, a young genet cat and a baby vervet monkey.

How we came by the baby porcupine was another lesson for the young lions. One bright morning, I walked with the three of them up a streambed not far from Tawana Camp. It was still cool and despite just failing to kill an impala, the lions remained on the move, hunting, eyes watchful and movements deliberate. As I followed them, I saw Furaha pause and then slowly stalk towards a small but thick bush. Rafiki and Batian then moved to surround the bush, peering into it. I then heard a loud rattle of quills which signalled that a porcupine had been cornered.

The lions began pawing through the branches, leaping excitedly whenever there was a sharp rattle of quills accompanied by stamping sounds. (The stamping of feet, I discovered, is part of a porcupine's defence display.) Suddenly a large porcupine rushed down a nearby burrow. Batian ran over to the hole and peered in. Turning back, I noticed that another porcupine remained within the bush with three tiny babies beneath her.

At this point, Batian was beginning to dig enthusiastically after the porcupine in the hole. However, he was inexperienced in the defensive ways of these animals and, after digging for a while, he plunged his head into the hole and sprang away with a loud grunt. Three or four sharp black and white quills were protruding from his head and, in his discomfort, he began to pull the quills free with his paws. Bleeding, but with this achieved, he abandoned the porcupine in the hole and went to join his sisters who were attempting to reach the mother and her young.

The female porcupine tried bravely to defend her young, but eventually scuttled out of the bush with quills rattling, leaving her babies behind. She ran down a streambed followed by Rafiki. The babies were now exposed. Batian quickly killed one and then began, in typical cat-and-mouse fashion, playing with the second. Furaha stood nearby pinning the third baby to the ground with her front left paw. I moved forward, feeling saddened by the babies' plight, and attracted Furaha's attention towards Batian. Quietly, as she stepped in his direction, I removed the baby porcupine from under her paw and carried it away. It was tiny, a mere six inches long, with the remains of an umbilical cord still visible.

I had a walkie-talkie with me which linked me to our main CB radio at the camp. I called Julie on the radio and told her to meet me on a road nearby. This she did and her maternal instincts rose at the sight of the baby cupped in my hands. We called the baby 'Noko', a rather unoriginal name as it simply means 'porcupine' in Setswana. In time, this name evolved to 'Nugu', meaning 'monkey' in Swahili, which suited his playful nature.

It was one thing rescuing Noko from the lions, but how does one feed and raise such a tiny porcupine? Initially, Julie adapted a syringe as a teat and bottle and fed Noko with an excellent cereal product called Pronutro. Fortunately the little one quickly took to the cereal food to which we added a small amount of diluted milk. To start with, the feeding sessions were messy affairs with more Pronutro ending up on Julie than inside Noko. In time, though, he began to feed himself from a bowl and from that point onwards, he never looked back. In fact, he became a voracious consumer of everything and had a penchant for junk foods, especially biscuits and crisps.

A very close bond developed between Julie and Noko and, in his bouncy quill-quivering way, he would follow her around the camp. Noko grew rapidly, but even when he was grown, he still loved to be lifted and cuddled by Julie. On these occasions, he would relax his quills into a flat position so that Julie was not harmed.

As Noko entered sub-adulthood, Julie and I discussed returning him to his natural home – the wilds. We could not do this from our camp because we were afraid the lions would find him. Instead, with much sadness but in the belief that we were doing what was best for Noko, we moved him to a friend's camp where he was to become adapted to the wilds.

It is now over two years since I rescued Noko from beneath Furaha's paw. From time to time, Noko still ventures into our friend's camp and has been seen on occasions with another porcupine. Presumably Noko has found a mate.

Once or twice a week in the early days of the project, Julie would set out in our vehicle for Pont Drift, the Botswana and South African border post on the Limpopo river, to make telephone calls and collect supplies. The drive down the Pitsani valley on to the plains that lead to the Limpopo and the border would normally take her an hour and fifteen minutes. At times, it would take her considerably longer, depending on the amount of 'elephant traffic' she encountered on the way. Sometimes great herds of elephant would block the road and Julie would be forced to wait patiently at a distance while the elephants proceeded with their leisurely feeding and eventually moved off, allowing Julie to continue safely with her journey. The elephants have right of way in the Tuli bushlands. If approached too closely, a matriarch cow, in fierce protection of her family and young, might charge, screaming in a storming rush towards the vehicle. Such charges are rarely fuelled with real intent to damage the vehicle or its occupants, though vehicles have been struck. It is, however, unfair for the elephants to undergo such stress caused purely by rash or inconsiderate behaviour by a driver.

Pont Drift is a small gateway to the bushlands. It is where tourists in their khaki garb are collected by the game guides and driven to the game lodges, and it is where they are returned after their safari. Upon reaching the borderpost's white building, Julie would again be back in the world of people. The Botswana borderpost officials came to know us well and we them. They would always enquire of Julie as to the lions' and my well-being and here too, Julie would meet, greet and chat to other people who lived and worked in the bushlands – the game guides, the private reserve managers and their staff.

To continue on to make her telephone calls, Julie would complete immigration formalities and drive across the empty Limpopo river, up on to its South African banks to a large shed made of corrugated metal sheeting. This was the cable-car shed where our telephone was locked up in a tin trunk attached to the wall. During the summer months, the Limpopo would flood with storm waters. At these times, the only way of crossing to and from Botswana is in a cable car which is swung across the river, above the swirling brown waters – a novel, if not unique, way of crossing an international boundary in Africa. Sitting on the wooden planks of the floor of the cable-car shed, Julie would make our phone calls.

In time, as our work began attracting media interest, the telephone linked us with people in faraway places. It was from here – the cable-car shed on the banks of the Limpopo – that we were interviewed for radio, newspapers and magazines by journalists in Australia, Britain and the United States, and it was often hard to imagine journalists taking notes in offices in cities, in another world so far distant from the Tuli bushlands and so far removed from our situation.

Sometimes I would have to call my literary agent, Tony Peake, in London. On these occasions, and knowing that he would enjoy it, I would tell him with relish what it had entailed to get to the phone to call him – perhaps having had to manoeuvre my way through a herd of two hundred elephants or, during the summer rains, having had to wade or swim across the Limpopo because the cable car had broken down. There was always a sense of unreality in speaking to Tony from a blisteringly hot cable-car shed in Africa while thousands of miles to the north, as snowflakes fell outside his home in London, he sat comfortably in his study.

After completing her calls, Julie would normally drive into the northern Transvaal to a small town called Alldays where she would buy fuel and supplies. The entire undertaking of a phone and supply trip would take Julie six hours or more.

As already mentioned, during the course of these trips, Julie would meet other inhabitants of the Tuli bushlands, often old friends and colleagues of mine from the days when I had worked in the area previously. One afternoon, she drove into Tawana Camp and said, 'Guess who I saw today? Fish Maila, and he wants to meet up with you soon.' I had not seen this softly spoken Motswana friend of mine for over three years. Now again back in the Tuli bushlands, I longed to renew my friendship with him.

Fish had been my tracker in the past. We had a friendship which had been built up over hours spent together in the bush as we introduced the wilds and its inhabitants to visitors to the game lodge where we both worked. As young men, Fish and I had experienced a great deal in the wilds together. My study of the Tuli lions at that time had been undertaken jointly with Fish in the sense that much of what I learnt of the lions and their circumstances would not have been possible without Fish's great knowledge of the Tuli bushlands and his tracking skills. I had learnt much from him, and he had learnt from me the tourism side of our work, the conducting of game drives and the handling of visitors of all nationalities who visited the wilds.

Together we had experienced some unnerving and at times dangerous encounters. On one occasion, we accidentally walked into an entire pride of sixteen lions. For ten slow minutes and in thick bush, we had stood our ground fifteen paces away from the threatening, annoyed lionesses of the pride. Together we had been charged by lions; we had been chased on numerous occasions by the then very aggressive Tuli elephants, and together we had nearly walked into concealed leopards.

I remember once with Fish that we came across the burrows of a hyena clan. We left the vehicle and walked around the site in search of fresh signs of any inhabitants. As I looked cautiously down into a burrow, a terrible mask of a face with a blunt head and teeth bared suddenly materialised from the gloom. On seeing this, I fled, leaving Fish somewhere behind me. Our strong camaraderie broke down that day as I ran to the vehicle. When I drove back to the burrows, I became concerned about Fish, who was conspicuous by his absence. I then spied one of his boots on the ground, then his hat and then a little further on, another boot. Worried, I began calling his name, and to my immense relief, I heard a muffled reply in the distance. Eventually, slightly embarrassed, my intrepid tracker emerged from the riverbed, hatless and unshod. While we laughed together, he explained what had happened. As the hyena had stuck its face out at me, unbeknown to him another had emerged from the burrow behind him. He had heard a sound, turned and come face to face with a hyena a mere two paces from where he stood. Instinctively, he had jumped back, kicked off his boots, thrown his prized hat at the terrifying sight and fled down towards the river as fast as his legs could carry him.

44

On another occasion, we had an alarming encounter with a black mamba. One afternoon, Fish and I were driving along in the bush in our open vehicle (which had no roof, no doors, etc.) when I turned a corner and saw a gunmetal-grey snake about three metres long lying across the entire width of the road. I swerved to avoid the mamba, but one of the tyres must have clipped its tail. Fish was sitting in the passenger seat and was nearest to the snake. He leapt on to my side as we heard the thud of the snake striking the vehicle. Then, with eyes wide, we watched a spectacle which I had always thought was a myth. The mamba tore off in a gliding motion through the bush, its head raised approximately five feet off the ground. It was an awesome, heart-stopping sight.

On yet another occasion, Fish and I were camping in the bush while we were attempting to lure livestock-killing lions back into the reserve when I was stung by a highly venomous scorpion. Fish and I had arrived back at our temporary camp, exhausted from a day of tracking the lions. As I sank wearily to the ground next to our fire, I felt an excruciating pain on the side of my leg. I jumped up and, in the light of the fire, I saw a small dark form scuttle away. 'Scorpion,' Fish said to me. 'A bad one, Gareth.' Despite the pain, I foolishly tried to make light of the situation. I had been stung by scorpions before and although on those occasions the pain had been bad, I could still carry on with my work. However, Fish had immediately recognised the dangerous type of scorpion which had just stung me. He straightaway insisted on driving me to the camp where we lived and said I would have to see the doctor. The pain increased as we set off on the hour's drive.

Dangerous scorpions can generally be distinguished by their very thick tails and slender pincers while, in contrast, mildly poisonous scorpions have large, powerful pincers and slim tails. I later learnt that the one that had stung me was from the genus *Parabuthus*, several species of which are potentially lethally toxic to man. Some have the additional ability to squirt their venom in the form of a fine spray up to a distance of over a metre. On entering a human eye, the venom causes very painful conjunctivitis similar to that caused by the venom of spitting snakes.

At the camp, I was given various treatments, but I had been stung badly. That night, I experienced terrible sweating and several times had great difficulty breathing. The following morning, with Fish,

I was driven to the nearest doctor in Alldays. I remember Fish watching me with grave concern, the thought that I may succumb to the venom clearly written on his face. However, after the doctor's treatment, I gradually recovered, but for over a week after the bite, I had difficulty drinking. It had certainly been a case of learning through experience, and I am indebted to Fish for recognising the seriousness of this particular scorpion's bite and for getting me to help so promptly.

This incident gave me a healthy respect for scorpions, so I remember Fish surprising me with incredible deftness of hand one night when he seized a large *Parabuthus* scorpion by the tail. While holding this venomous creature between his finger and thumb, he demonstrated how to extract the venom from its tail. This was old knowledge, now being taught to me, knowledge that had been passed to Fish by a member of a Bushman clan with whom he had lived years ago. Bushmen are expert toxicologists and concoct poisons with which they tip their arrow-heads. These poisons, which in certain areas include the poison of the *Parabuthus*, are capable of severely weakening even large animals such as giraffe to the point where the little hunters can approach and spear them to death. No known antidote can save either animals or man from such Bushman poisons.

Shortly after he'd seen Julie at Pont Drift, I saw Fish while I was driving to the border. Now a game guide and smart in his uniform, he was driving a safari vehicle filled with tourists. We were both very excited to meet one another again after three long years and I was proud of his new status. After I had left my job at the game lodge, Fish had deservedly been promoted from tracker to game guide and had taken over my position. Today he is the most experienced game guide in that private reserve.

Meeting Fish again soon after that first brief encounter, I told him what I was trying to do for Batian, Rafiki and Furaha. I wanted to share it with him and invited him to visit my camp, which he did. One evening, I introduced him to the lions as they came into their enclosure. The lions seemed to like Fish, sniffing and peering inquisitively as they came to the fence while we sat next to the enclosure. That night, I asked Fish if he would accompany me and the lions the following day on one of our exploratory excursions – something even Julie had not experienced. Without hesitation, Fish accepted.

Early the following morning, we walked out of the camp and I opened the gate of the lions' enclosure. The lions gambolled out and curiously approached Fish. Then, caught up with their natural youthful exuberance, they stepped ahead of us. Fish and I spent a wonderful morning with the lions and their acceptance of him was complete. He in turn expressed no apprehension about walking amongst the young pride. I captured this day of sharing – a day which was to me a culmination of our past experiences – in a photograph I took that morning. It shows Fish standing quite at ease amongst two of the lions as one peered down at him from the large branch of a tree. It was a day I will not forget and one Fish will always remember fondly. My trust in the lions and vice versa reflected from them to Fish.

The only sadness of the day was knowing that it would never be repeated. Defamiliarisation with people was essential if the lions' rehabilitation was to be a success. I would have given a lot for Fish to have joined me in my work, but after much pondering I felt this would perhaps be counter-productive. He was a highly respected game guide with a stable job, a job he had worked hard to get. In addition, I knew that I could not afford to pay him a salary on a par with what he was earning. For many reasons, I did not mention my thoughts to him as I drove with him away from camp after his stay. Realistically, I knew that for the lions' sake, I needed an assistant to accompany me into the bush with them, for who would continue with the work if something happened to me? Fortunately, no accident was fated in the rehabilitation stage of our project.

Time passed, and today as I write this, I have still not been able to pass on the knowledge I have gained in lion rehabilitation first-hand. I am about to co-author a paper on the processes of rehabilitation and the physical and behavioural development of young lions – but, again, this is not passing on the knowledge in a practical way. Julie knows the principles, but did not experience what was involved out in the bush in the practical sense. Fish was to me the only possible suitable candidate because of his depth of knowledge of animal behaviour and his relationship with me. It would have been right if Fish could have been the recipient of what I have learnt. It would have been a rightful exchange for all the knowledge I had gained from him.

CHAPTER

4

Lion Life

The hottest months in the Tuli are those at the end and beginning of the year, with Christmas temperatures soaring as high as forty-nine degrees in the shade, and substantially more in the sun. The lions were seventeen months old as our first Christmas in the Tuli together approached. Rafiki and Furaha would have weighed some 70–80 kilograms, with Batian being perhaps 15 kilograms heavier. Furaha had, at this stage, developed a very noticeable devotion to her brother, always lying next to him when they rested. Rafiki, though, found much comfort in my presence. As Furaha would do with Batian, she would always lie beside me when we stopped to rest in the shade during our exploratory wanderings in the bush. Rafiki and I were forming a strong bond which exists, unweakened, to this day.

Our daily routine found us leaving on our walks between four thirty and five each morning. By ten o'clock, the heat would have sapped the lions' enthusiasm to continue any longer with their exploring and hunting. On these hot days, we would lie up in the shade until the temperatures began to drop in the afternoon.

On our walks at this time, I noticed that the lions were beginning to show signs of expressing ownership of 'their' range area. The lion society is divided into resident prides with defined though seasonally shifting range areas, and nomads, distinguishable from residents by their lack of a stable pride composition and range, and by the way in which individuals join up with other wanderers, parting at loose intervals. Generally, a stable resident pride is basically made up of lionesses, all of which are genetically related – sisters, aunts, etc. Resident males provide security to the group and particularly to cubs until, after some time, they are ousted by prideless males, nomads, who then have their period of residency and so the cycle continues. Lions can advertise their resident status and ownership of an area in various ways, making their presence known to other lions. This can be done by 'calling', the so-called lion's roar, which advertises an individual or pride's presence across many kilometres, but also by leaving signs of their presence as they roam. Adult males deliver well-aimed squirts of urine, scented from an anal gland, backwards into bushes. Lionesses can do the same, but generally squat, urinate and scrape at the ground. By so doing, lions can constantly exchange information, warning any wanderers who may be venturing too deeply into a resident pride's range.

I noticed Batian acting out 'squirting'. He would first rub his head against branches and leaves in low bushes before turning around with his tail raised. Occasionally this was accompanied by him scraping at the ground with his hind feet. Furaha and Rafiki would also scrape and I too would go through the marking ritual (though obviously not as thoroughly as the lions) to demonstrate my own unity with the young pride. At times when I acted out scent-marking and jetting, my actions would stimulate one or all of the lions to do likewise. Such actions became so much part of our lives together that at times I was not sure who was prompting who to scent-mark as it seemed to take place automatically.

I dearly wished my lions to become territorial as quickly as poss-ible. If they did not feel secure within the vicinity of Tawana and their growing range, they might, as they progressed into sub-adulthood, become wanderers, nomads. This would be a great danger as, being unprofilic at hunting, their hunger might lead them into the livestock areas on the Tuli's western and eastern boundaries – areas where obvious dangers, posed by man, lay.

My provision of a sense of security in the lions, and my deepening bond with them due to hours of interaction and togetherness, in part created a situation from which their eventual full territoriality was to develop. The lions did not face any major competition for their range, although skirmishes with other lions did occasionally occur. I had chosen the Tawana and Pitsani valleys specifically for the rehabilitation project because I anticipated no wild lions being resident in that area, and therefore no real competition for my lions being present. This, in one sad sense, proved to be a correct assumption. The past effects of poaching in the Tawana area had created a 'lion-less' vacuum which had not been recolonised by other lions, primarily, as I later discovered, due to the unstable situation in the numbers of the Tuli lion population. George Adamson's lions were, in reality, taking the place of the resident lions of the past, recolonising a prime but empty pride area left behind by the poachers.

On our early walks, I would not uncommonly come across poachers' snares dangling loose to the ground, broken by some unfortunate animal. Other snares I found were sometimes still set and, upon discovering them, I was chilled with the fear that one of my young lions could walk into such a trap. These snares, coupled with the lack of signs of resident lions, further indicated to me that the overall Tuli lion population had not risen during the three and a half years I had been away from the area. I only learnt of the full effects of the poaching still taking place in the months ahead.

Being with the lions over such long periods of time continued to allow me to witness further unusual encounters between them and other animals in the Tuli. The most dangerous of these encounters occurred early in the new year in an incident between the lions, an adult male leopard and me.

But there were other animals that I observed with the lions in the last weeks of 1989. Jackals are often seen in association with lions, most commonly when a pride has made a kill. Jackals are also sometimes observed trailing behind a pride, anticipating that at some point they will hunt and in turn the jackal will receive his share after the lions have fed.

On our walks, near a low hill which I had named 'Cub Koppie' and which overlooked a long plain, we would often encounter a pair of jackals. Initially, due to my presence, the jackals would scamper away from a distance. In time, however, they became less shy and at times almost bold. Some mornings while I rested with the lions, the jackal pair would potter around eyeing us. I imagined them trying to will us to hunt and kill. When we moved off, they would sometimes move forward to sniff at where we had lain, then follow us for a while.

Sadly, the relationship between us and the jackals ended abruptly. One windy morning, we left Cub Koppie heading south and unusually had not seen the jackal pair. As we entered an area of scrubby, stunted mopane trees, I noticed a movement ahead of me. Over the past weeks, whenever I spotted an animal before the lions did, I always stopped and crouched, signalling to the pride that potential prey lay ahead. On this occasion, I instinctively did this and then saw that it was the jackal couple foraging about ahead of us. By the time I realised this, Furaha and Rafiki had immediately stopped at my signal. Peering ahead, they had seen the jackals and Rafiki broke away to move, close to the ground, in a sweeping, half-circle hunting movement. Furaha, step after deliberate step, stalked forward and then charged. At this, I stood upright and watched as both jackals ran in swift figures of eight to avoid being caught. The jackals had not known Rafiki's position and the male was seized by her as his mate escaped. As she had done with the monitor lizard, Rafiki bit the jackal through the lower spine. Its hindquarters went limp while it still moved its mouth and front legs in convulsive jerks. After approximately ten minutes and after it had been carried away to different bushes and 'played with', the jackal died.

Again the lions had gained valuable experience through the hunt and the 'lion' side of me was pleased, while the other part of me felt sadness. That night in my tent, I did not hear the duet call of the jackal pair from Cub Koppie. Only a single jackal called, a strange, lamenting cry of the now lone female.

For some weeks I would spot the female near Cub Koppie walking alone and to me she appeared forlorn. But it has been said that 'nature abhors a vacuum' and, one morning, I came across the female with another male – and I smiled.

There was one other predator that I would often see while with the lions and he too followed us in a seemingly opportunistic manner. However, he was beyond the reach of even the lions – a young Bateleur eagle. Batty, as I called him, would fly over us in widening circles in the blue above. Bateleur eagles are perhaps the most majestic flyers of all the African raptors, tilting each wing slightly as they glide otherwise effortlessly on the rising thermals. Bateleurs are also great scavengers, often finding a kill before even the vultures do, and they are said to consume the eyeballs of the dead before the more powerful raptors, like the lappet-faced vultures, arrive to open up a carcass. Bateleurs are also one of the few birds that can successfully scavenge from a leopard's kill draped in the fork of a tree. The vultures, being large and cumbersome, cannot, like the Bateleur, swoop down and under the canopy of a tree to where a leopard's kill may be slung on a branch. In the wilds, seeing such interactions emphasised to me how clearly every single species has a specific and important role in the intricate workings of nature.

Batty represented true freedom, aloft in the skies, gliding the thermals, looking down at the strange procession of a man and three lions on the hot ground who were seeking shade. Sometimes I would call to him. Once, as the lions and I rested beneath a Shepherds tree, I heard a swoop of wings and an object landing on the branch of a nearby gnarled dead tree. I looked up as the lions awoke with a start from their slumbers, and there was Batty just metres away. He was checking, I presume, to see if a kill existed in the shade of the tree where we lay. A few minutes later, curiosity satisfied, he swooped away, and four heads lifted as we watched him return to his limitless domain in the skies.

As my lions were showing increasing signs of establishing a territory in the Tawana and Pitsani valleys, an incident occurred which ensured all scent-marking and jetting stopped for a while. The old pride male from the Lower Majale pride had arrived at Tawana, roaring, jetting and acting threateningly. Six years previously, I had named this lion Darky. He was a magnificent black-maned male with a slatey grey coat.

Early in the morning, fourteen days before Christmas, with the lions within their fenced enclosure, Julie and I awoke to the noise of a lion roaring loudly just beyond the perimeter of the camp's fence. It was still pitch-black as I groped for my torch and then swung its beam into the cubs' enclosure. They were clearly terrified by the presence of the wild lion roaring nearby and were huddled together at a point in their enclosure closest to my tent. I called to the three softly to comfort them, then turned the torch in the direction of the perimeter fence – and there was Darky. He loomed large and menacingly, staring in at me and the three young lions. He then walked alongside the fence towards the small gate of the cubs' enclosure and, to his right, I saw other lions – females and a single cub.

Although for years I had loved old Darky, I was suddenly consumed by a fierce protectiveness for my lions. I ran towards the fence, shouting at him and the pride aggressively. To my astonishment, the lion did not flee but, rumbling like a storm's beginnings, roared back at me in the typical loud, drawn-out lion manner. I shouted again, shining the torch towards the pride and again they called back. Only after some time did they move away into the scrubby bush. Darky, however, remained and my three lions stayed clumped together in a tawny heap. Darky moved towards some mopane bushes and jetted vigorously, scraping the ground with his powerful hind legs.

I continued to shout and, while doing so, somehow the youngsters in the enclosure separated. Darky surprised one of them – Furaha – who was by the fence. She darted away, grunting, and I was astonished to see Batian rush a short distance towards Darky in an attempt to defend his sister. This was a remarkably brave act for a seventeen-month-old lion who, at that stage, was probably half the old veteran's weight.

When Darky eventually moved away, I sat with my three lions. Rafiki, the most terrified, was respiring in a series of short, hiccuping breaths. I stayed with them until sunrise. Then, much later in the day, alone I tracked and found old Darky ten kilometres south, once again deep within his Lower Majale territory.

Fortunately, such visits by Darky were very rare, and in the months ahead and once Batian had matured to the extent that he too could roar like an adult male, Darky stayed in the south. This surprised me considering the age and size difference between them but nevertheless it was a welcome and pleasant surprise.

For many days after Darky's visit, Batian and his sisters refrained from any scent-marking and when they did begin again, it was initially in a very half-hearted fashion.

Darky was at this time a very old male lion, a living legend in the Tuli, a lion who, over the years, had been sighted and viewed by thousands of tourists and visitors. In a well-balanced lion population, a male such as Darky would normally only reign as pride male for three to four years before being ousted by other males. In such cases, the original males usually disappear, and do not live much beyond the age of eight to ten years.

At the time of the incident at Tawana, Darky was estimated to be between fourteen and sixteen years old, an exceptional age. I had known Darky first in 1983 when, even then, he was a fully grown pride master of the Lower Majale and ranged in a territory of some seventy to a hundred square kilometres. Tragically, the old man, over the years, had lost a number of his pride; his fellow pride male, Kgosi, his pride females, daughters and sons to the poachers' wire snares and the South African farmers. Somehow, Darky survived while his pride dwindled and it seemed that he was blessed with more than a cat's 'nine lives'. However, Darky did not escape the dangers entirely. He was once caught around his neck and great mane by a poacher's snare made from thick cable wire. Darky fought the snare, biting his way free, but in doing so, he snapped his top and bottom right canines on the metal. Dr Andrew McKenzie, a veterinary friend of mine, later tranquillised Darky to remove the wire that still remained around his great neck. The trauma which Darky experienced when caught in the snare must have been immense.

When I first began my study of the Tuli lions in 1983, Darky was one of the first lions I began to know well. He taught me much about his kind and became like a totem to me. At that time, I wrote the following words less than an hour after a magical encounter with Darky, at a time when a strange closeness that developed between us was at its strongest:

The sun had not yet risen before I heard his bellowing call floating towards me on the early morning breeze. He was moving steadily south along the banks of the dry Majale river, his footfalls muffled by the yielding soft brown soil. He called again across the land as I drew nearer. His voice awoke the antelope from their sun-seeking stillness and upon the hillsides for miles around the animals momentarily turned their heads in the direction of the haunting song.

I found his track, exaggerated in size upon the silky dust, as yet unblemished by the busy doves which pattered quickly round in frenzied circles on the fresh morning earth. His pawprints lay in front of me like a line of broken flowers, his splayed toes encircling the heavy back pad. I then walked as he walked, exactly where he moved in the morning light. I breathed his breath which rolled and swirled in the air towards me. I followed his steps to where he had paused. I felt the wetness upon the low bush dripping with warm urine, like dew upon the leaves, splashing slowly on to the insatiable dry winter soil, drying quickly into dark brown spots.

I felt his presence strongly and close. Ahead of me lay a crumbling bank and as I moved forward a jackal whined, as if in pain, from a few hidden paces away.

Kudu ewes, striped, and poised for flight, broke suddenly from the acacia cover, barking as they do only when lion is near. I followed his tracks and saw how he had used the mud bank for concealment, occasionally rising to survey the kudu below.

I entered the thicket and he was close. He watched. I had been seen. He turned his shaggy dark head and stared at my approaching figure. He moved to the right and then stopped again to stare with amber eyes before moving in a half-circle, partly out of a need of concealment and partly out of curiosity. I did not see him, but did not need to as I felt the power of his eyes. I knew Darky well, and strangely, although I knew he was near and was watching, I felt no fear, only a primitive feeling of awe at his presence.

I lost his tracks in a criss-cross of leaves and twigs and slowly returned to where I had last seen them. There, not minutes before I returned, stood Darky, tall, heavy, grey and watching. I checked my footprints as I approached that spot and over my crumbling bootprint lay the tracks of his mighty paws. I then moved instinctively towards the safer, more open country and from a few paces away, concealed by the bush, he watched. I moved like early man, walking unconsciously and instinctively towards the security of the visual openness of the plains, away from the dark thicket of his domain.

Darky had avoided, not harassed, me; he had seen my being, but had not attacked; his thoughts had been controlled and not aggressive.

I returned from this primitive experience to the present. I walked to my vehicle and he silently returned to his world which, perhaps, he had never left.

Inexplicably, in 1986, just when I had made the decision to leave the Tuli to write *Cry for the Lions* to publicise the plight of Darky and all the Tuli lions, the old male sought to attack me.

In this incident, he came for me while I was tracking him on foot, charging from where he lay unseen over a hundred and fifty metres away. I had had my back to him and was walking away when he crashed towards me. When, in his charge, he was less than thirty metres away, I had to resort to firing a shot over his head. He turned and spun away.

The charge had taken place in the centre of his core area and I can only interpret his actions, after knowing Darky for so long, as being that he was ousting me from his area. The lion who had taught me so much had, I feel, acted to chase me from his land for a definite reason. It may sound fanciful, my interpreting that the old man was chasing me away as he would one of his sub-adult sons, but it is strange that for the next three years I went through a nomadic stage as a young male lion would do – maturing, learning, travelling vast distances, with no fixed abode. Strange too that I should eventually return to the Tuli, with much knowledge gained, to establish my own pride in the land where my understanding of lions had been born.

In time, Batian developed into a pride male, seeing me as his fellow pride male, and it is another coincidence that Batian, that side of me, later almost became the new master of Darky's Lower Majale pride.

Lions and leopards are natural competitors and rivals. If an opportunity arises, lions will attack and kill leopards (and cheetah). In turn, leopards will kill unattended lion cubs and, it has been reported, kill and eat young cheetah.

A lion's drive to attack leopard is, I discovered, instinctive, and not learned behaviour passed on by mother to cub. It is a very strong trait and therefore must serve an important purpose in the natural balance between these big cats. The behaviour is not dictated in any way by hunger, as after a leopard has been killed, lions rarely more than mouth at the body.

Early in the new year, my lions' first and most dramatic encounter with a leopard occurred when they were just eighteen months old, technically termed at that age as 'large cubs'. Rafiki and Furaha at the time would have weighed some seventy kilograms while Batian was probably fifteen kilograms heavier than his two sisters.

While walking with the lions east of Cub Koppie one morning, I came across the fresh tracks of a large male leopard. As I bent down to inspect the tracks, Batian approached and nosed at the area where the tracks lay imprinted upon the soft red soil. I watched with curiosity as a little later all three lions walked purposefully in the direction in which the tracks led. As this took them towards a shady area where at times we would rest during the day, I began to think that the lions were merely moving to the shade. They passed through this area and were, in fact, partially by scent, searching for the leopard.

I followed behind and as I stepped up on to a stream's bank, I suddenly heard loud snarling and coarse growling. I looked up to see Batian and Furaha hoisting themselves up a Shepherds tree, on the topmost part of which stood a leopard. At the lions' advance, the leopard leapt out of the tree from a height of some four metres, hit the ground and raced away. With the lions pursuing it, the leopard ran for perhaps seventy metres before leaping into a small, low mopane tree just five metres high.

I watched hidden in the background as the lions renewed their attack upon the leopard, standing upright on their hind legs and then clawing their way up the small tree to swipe and snarl at it. The noise, I imagine, could be heard for kilometres around, those deep, menacing sounds echoing throughout the nearby valley.

As it desperately defended itself, the leopard occasionally defecated, marking the lions below with its black, tar-like faeces. The scene which I was witnessing was a fight for life, a fight for death, necessary violence in one of its most basic forms in the African wilds.

After some twenty minutes, the leopard jumped out of the flimsy tree, leaping without much leverage as far as possible over the lions. It landed clumsily, winding itself, but somehow managed to run on towards a streambed. The lions followed immediately. By the time I reached the streambed, the leopard had backed itself into a low bush and was surrounded by the lions. The fight continued as the heat grew increasingly intense. I saw the leopard lie on its back in its last defence posture, flailing with paws and jaws at the lions. Later I thought the leopard was mortally injured, particularly as one by one the lions moved away to rest in some nearby shade.

The leopard now lay in the streambed, scarcely moving. I joined the panting and bloodied lions in the shade. To my astonishment, just as I sat down, I noticed the leopard turn over, rise to its feet and, with its head low, begin gingerly moving away. This movement did not escape the lions who rose and rushed at the leopard.

Surrounded, the leopard lay again on its back. Batian approached it from the front and was caught on the nose and around the eyes by two tearing swipes of the leopard's paws. Hurt, Batian then retaliated with great force, using a level of power previously not used in the fray. He crashed his paws, claws exposed, on to the head of the leopard in a series of enormously powerful and heavy blows – left, right, left, right . . .

After this attack, Batian moved away and left the leopard seemingly stunned, its eyes unfocused, its movements uncoordinated. He then lay down, leaving his sisters to watch the leopard. The tremendous force behind his blows to the leopard had been the result of pure anger after being hurt. It was a rare demonstration of Batian showing his power and violence due to anger and pain.

The fight continued on spasmodically. Furaha too was caught by the slashing paws of the leopard. Its claws split the soft, black skin around her mouth and blood dripped on to her chin and white chest. She left the leopard to Rafiki and moved away to rest.

When I saw the blood on Furaha's mouth and chin, I called softly to her from where I was hidden on the bank of the streambed behind some bushes. Furaha turned, headed towards me, then sat beside me facing towards where the leopard lay. I pulled a water-bottle out of the bag I was carrying and poured water into my hand. In spite of Furaha having been hurt and feeling hot, she allowed me to stroke her, to wash her wounds and inspect the gashes and tears on her mouth. Then she drank some water from my cupped hand, which I replenished several times.

The leopard at this point was lying practically motionless in the dry, exposed streambed in the furnace-like heat. I thought that the leopard might be nearing death, having been bitten, I noticed, on many parts of its body including its stomach. This perception was soon to be proven very wrong.

As I got up into a semi-crouched position to put the water-bottle back into the bag, the leopard, thirty metres away, saw me for the first time. Furaha sat next to me, watching the leopard from the bank.

Without warning, the leopard, in one quick motion, suddenly spun on to its feet and charged towards me. I instinctively rose and rammed a bullet in the rifle's breech at the same time. The leopard was now leaping up on to the bank and was less than three metres away when suddenly I saw Furaha launch herself, in a blur of gold, across me and land on the leopard, causing it to be knocked over and then pulled down the bank.

I leapt three or four paces back, abandoning my bag, but keeping my rifle held high. I continued moving backwards with Furaha and the leopard now out of vision, but I could hear tremendous growling below me. Then I saw Rafiki and Batian bounding towards where Furaha and the leopard fought.

From a distance, I later saw the leopard lying on its back, surrounded once again by all three lions. I walked to camp to collect my camera, and later in the day returned to the vicinity of the fight. I stopped a hundred metres away and listened, hearing no sounds of fighting. Was the leopard dead or alive? As I was uncertain, I called Batian, feeling that if I went into the streambed with him, I would be reasonably safe.

Batian emerged, followed by Rafiki, and both greeted me affectionately. I felt they sensed my feelings, and Batian walked beside me as I headed towards the streambed. He then led the way, heading towards a thick bush, and stopped to paw beneath it. There lay the leopard, its eyes staring wide but unseeing. It was dead. I began to pull the leopard from beneath the bush into the open. Batian joined me in this task, hooking his claws into its fur and walking and tugging backwards.

The leopard, I realised, had been in its prime – over two metres long and weighing I estimated, at least sixty kilograms. It had been killed by a deep bite through the nape of its neck, presumably from Batian's jaws.

By persistently pursuing, fighting and eventually killing the leopard, Batian, Rafiki and Furaha had exposed their wild lion hearts, risking injury to assert their dominance over the leopard. It was an extraordinary encounter, particularly since, to my knowledge, this must have been one of the first leopards they had ever seen.

As the sun lowered, the lions and I moved away, leaving the leopard where it lay, and headed back to the camp. As my scratched and bloodied trio drank thirstily from the water-bowls in their enclosure, a great fiery glow spread in the sky, marking the end of the day. It had been a dramatic and important day in which the lions' continued development had been vividly illustrated.

Julie was away that night. I was eager for her return the following day so that I could tell her of the lions' achievement.

The next morning, I accompanied the lions on a walk and, as they rested, I returned to the site of the fight. The ground was littered with the tracks of hyena and jackal. I searched for the leopard's remains, but nearly all was gone, consumed by the meat-eaters. Only some dry droplets of blood on the stones and tufts of fur caught on fallen branches indicated that there a leopard had fought and died just a day before. The scene of so much noise, power and life now seemed empty and hollow. I stood there a while reflecting on how, if it had not been for Furaha's actions, my blood too could have spilled at this place.

Living such an intense life within a pride occasionally gave me an unparalleled insight into the spirit of the lion, an animal that expresses such kinship, gentleness and affection within its pride, but is capable of extreme violence. Being part of life within a pride on occasions such as the leopard's death would cause me to ponder on my own mortality and the many shapes and faces of death here in the wilds.

With the lions, I was surrounded by so much life, but also much death. And so an awareness of death developed within me.

CHAPTER

5

Wild Ways and the Seasons Change

Our first Christmas with the lions in the Tuli was, in part, a joyous period, but it was permeated with melancholy undercurrents. Julie and I obviously felt great happiness being with the lions at this time of year, but celebrated their wonderful progress in the Tuli rather than the season itself.

Christmas evoked personal and deeply felt memories within us both. Julie's thoughts were with what had occurred the Christmas before when her father had passed away. She felt guilty because she was not with the rest of her family which had gathered round her mother. Julie had sacrificed the occasion so that I would not be alone in the Tuli at this time. On reflection, we both realised, even though I greatly appreciated her staying at Tawana, that she would have had a happier time being with her family rather than being burdened by guilt and haunted by memories of what had taken place exactly a year before.

My thoughts at this time were also dominated by memories of the previous Christmas, of being with George Adamson and the cubs at Kora. That had been George's last season of giving and I dwelt much on that time and what had occurred in the past year. Exactly a year before, I was on the verge of leaving Kora, George and the cubs. The parting was near and I felt then that I would never see George again. After that last Christmas, I never did.

I remember that last Kora Christmas well; in particular George giving the three cubs, then only five months old, a special feast – an entire goat's carcass. He did so before we sat down, in soaring temperatures and with perspiring faces, to enjoy the turkey, ham and pudding which George's old cook, Hamissi, had somehow produced from his ancient blackened pots upon a simple fire. Before we ate, George had called his staff to bring the goat's carcass for the cubs. Rafiki, Furaha and Batian sat unmoving, looking at the offering, apparently perplexed, before becoming excited and pouncing upon the carcass, acting out the killing of the goat. George, standing nearby, chuckled as he puffed upon his pipe. Never in their short lives had the cubs seen such a large amount of food. That Christmas day and night, the little ones ate heartily, and in the days that followed mostly lay on their backs and sides, appearing uncomfortably overindulged and looking like tawny, misshapen balloons in the sand.

Over that last Christmas, George took care to feed the rest of his wild family too – the birds, squirrels, monkeys and bushbabies – with special double rations. After our Christmas lunch, he spread out seeds for the guinea fowls, peanuts for the hornbills and squirrels. The vervet monkeys scurried up to him to receive their share. I remember watching the baby monkeys clinging to his fingers in absolute trust as they gently picked the offerings from his open palm.

As New Year's Eve neared, George withdrew increasingly into himself. It was approaching the ninth anniversary of the murder of his wife, Joy. In addition, George's wild pride – Growe, One Eye and the others – had not visited Kampi ya Simba for almost a month and this, I felt, added to his melancholy mood. He wished for his lions' reappearance for many reasons, one being that the lions gave him spiritual strength, the upliftment which he needed. Old people must ponder quietly as Christmas comes and goes as to whether they will again the following year celebrate another season of giving. However, this may not only be a preoccupation of old people since it is also a morbid (some would say) thought of mine each Christmas. Perhaps George dwelled privately on such thoughts, pondering his own immortality; his need for the presence of his lions, however, was clear and unmasked.

On the night of New Year's Eve, with the pride still unseen,

George and I sat with three young camp visitors, chatting, waiting to see the New Year in. Ten minutes before Big Ben's chimes were to ring from George's old radio which was tuned into a faraway London, a magical, emotional occurrence took place. George and I together suddenly felt – not seeing nor hearing, but feeling – the presence of a lion. George turned on his torch, shining it beyond the camp fence. There in the night stood old Growe, calmly, from the outside looking in.

Over those past days, George had needed her. In his mind he had called her . . . and now she had come. After greeting the grand old lady, George gave Growe some meat. While she fed, the champagne cork was popped and as the chimes rang out, we sang a disjointed version of 'Auld Lang Syne'. Only George knew all the words.

George's Christmas, his last, was now complete. With Growe concealed by darkness, but with her presence almost tangible, George rose from his seat. With a turned head, attempting to hide tears, he bade us a cheery goodnight, and then to Growe out there in the night, he bade a happy new year.

George wanted to celebrate privately. The emotion he felt was an emotion which one can only share with oneself. Like most important events in his life, George's last Christmas was sealed by the blessing of a lion. That, for the man who constantly gave, was all he wished for himself.

Such memories surrounded me as, a year later, I sat with his lions at Christmas time in the Tuli – and I wondered, where was Growe now?

The profusion of life – birth and rebirth – is dramatic during the time of the summer rains in the Botswana bushlands. This is a time of contrast and wonder. The Tuli, just prior to the rains, is a stark, dry place with the trees standing leafless and seemingly dead, the ground bare and dust blowing in the strong winds. The animals, particularly the antelope, are lacking vitality and are in poor condition, with ribs beginning to show through their once glossy coats. Prior to the eagerly awaited summer storms, no rain would have fallen for some five months or more.

There is, however, an air of excitement within the animals of the Tuli just as the grey and white stormheads rise from the south and grumble up above. The animals become almost filled with a sense

65

of anticipation of the rain to fall, skipping and leaping with energy which, for weeks previously, had seemed totally lacking. At this point, at this sign, the rain comes.

A drop, then another, falls heavily, then uncountable hundreds follow with increasing tempo as the minutes pass. The ground becomes saturated, small gulleys become filled and water slinks its way along the dips into the streambeds, the waters rising, and rising more, swirling, rushing southwards towards the great empty river below, the Limpopo. It fills and gives us a glimpse of its former glory.

At the beginning of our first rains in the Tuli, Julie and I too were caught up in the excitement and would stand outside, allowing ourselves to be drenched before – with the wind whipping around our bodies – we would be forced to rush into our small tent, gloriously and invigoratingly chilled to the bone for the first time in months. The rains had mercifully come.

During these rains, as the soil sucked up the water it would darken and within days a sheen of greenness would appear all around us. If sufficient rains had fallen, the Pitsani plains would first become tinged with green and only days later, thousands of tiny yellow flowers, known as 'Duiweltjies' (little devils), would open, transforming the stark lunar winter appearance of the plains into a blaze of yellow and green, like a great field carpeted exclusively with buttercups.

Triggered by the rains, new life would come in many forms; the opening of a flower, the budding of a new leaf, the hatching of eggs and emergence of chicks, and in the birth of many young mammals. Jackal cubs frolicked on the yellow plains, and baboons patiently picked at the flowers, eating each one individually and with relish, while sitting dotted on the swathes of gold and green.

My lions were also excited by the first rains. I remember once, as it began to hail, the lions dashing around, leaping on to each other and gradually turning from yellow to dark brown as the earth became mud. Their games continued until the sky began flinging large hailstones earthwards. The lions were stung by the ice and they became distracted from their games as the large stones bounded off their heads and bodies. All three lions fled into one of the crates in which they had been brought from Kenya. Julie and I laughed as we watched the lions as one bundle together into a crate designed, three months previously, for a single young lion. Tails and flanks protruded from the crate but, for the most part, the lions escaped the icy stones.

As the stream next to the camp filled during the first rains, the lions watched the rising waters with curiosity, apparently seeing the rushing flow as a living thing. It was Batian who cautiously first ventured towards the water. He slowly stretched out a front leg, then patted at the swirling waters. His sisters were more watchful of the stream and eventually only ventured forward when Batian was cavorting in the water. Admittedly, I had encouraged him as I had entered the stream calling him to follow. Later all three lions frolicked in the water, running along the shallow parts, chasing one another and revelling in the sounds of their paws crashing with spray on the water.

At that time, I remembered George once telling me at Kora how it amused him to see his lions avoiding puddles and when they did get their paws wet, shaking them indignantly, as a domestic cat does, but all the while knowing they would not hesitate to swim in and sometimes across the Tana river.

Batian clearly loved the filled streams and pans. It seemed he saw the rushing waters in the stream as a personal challenge. Repeatedly, he would swim across, climb on to the bank, study and pat the water before once again plunging in to cross the stream. The arrival of the first rains was a joyous time for all.

Along the banks of streambeds, where the vegetation had grown quickly, baby impala would be seen wobbling to their feet, then later would be hidden as their mothers moved away to feed. The profusion of these young antelope provided my lions with an increase in hunting opportunities and I remember clearly one of their first young impala kills.

On this occasion, the lions flushed a youngster from thick mopane bush and it was seized and killed by Rafiki. Perturbed by the presence of her brother and sister, she then commenced to drag her kill for over an hour in a large circle before resigning herself to their attendance and settling down to begin feeding. She did, however, growl loudly and lunge forward if either of the other two ventured too near to her. Batian and Furaha watched her constantly as she devoured the impala, waiting for their opportunity to feed too.

Rafiki's technique of feeding, I remember, was most odd. Lions characteristically begin feeding on the soft parts such as the belly. However, Rafiki would begin chewing on an ear and then, with this consumed, would begin on the head and progress downwards to the neck, then chest, etc. It was more like watching a python, rather than a lion, feeding.

When only two hind-leg bones remained, Rafiki suddenly skipped away and Batian and Furaha leapt forward to seize the extremely frugal remains. Apparently frustrated at the little his sister had left, Batian ran up to Rafiki and, to her obvious annoyance, began repeatedly slapping her with his front paws.

It was not long after this kill, during the early summer, that two highly unusual incidents occurred. The first was between the lions and a baboon, and the second between the lions and an elephant.

The baboon incident occurred one morning just after the lions and I had been playing in a stream and were walking away along its banks. Suddenly, ahead of us, we heard the alarm barks of a troupe of baboons. A chase followed, and a young male baboon found himself cut off from the fleeing troupe and bounded up an isolated leadwood tree. The lions peered up into the tree at the baboon and then began climbing the tree in an attempt to seize it. The baboon, I felt, was doomed as it had no nearby tree into which to leap to escape the lions. Somehow, the baboon managed to evade the lions for some time, jumping from branch to branch as the lions approached.

Rafiki grew tired of the hunt, or perhaps of the baboon's screams, and climbed down the tree, padding slowly away. Just at this point, Batian and Furaha pulled themselves particularly close to the terrified baboon, causing it to take drastic measures. It scampered a little downwards and along the furthermost limb before suddenly leaping into the air with the ground some five metres below.

Rafiki was directly below the falling baboon, totally unaware of what was hurtling earthwards above her. To this day, whenever I think of the incident, it is as though what I watched occurred in slow motion. The baboon fell directly on top of Rafiki, looking like an oversized jockey on a medium-sized mount. Rafiki stumbled, grunting in surprise and no doubt a certain amount of pain. The shocked baboon screamed, but somehow, in the confusion, managed to rush away. As if this were not enough for the baboon to endure, Batian and Furaha had jumped down from the tree and continued to pursue it. The baboon did, however, eventually escape. I wished it well.

The unusual incident with the elephant occurred only a week or so later. If I had not witnessed the incident myself, I would not have thought it possible. On this occasion, we were only two kilometres from the camp when the lions and I saw a herd of feeding elephants ahead. They were in an area of wonderously green and rain-revived mopane trees. The lions broke away to stalk the herd while I, with greater respect for the Tuli elephants, climbed up on to a cliff to be in a safe position if the elephants charged out of the thicket.

My caution was to no avail. As I climbed the cliff above the elephants, I discovered yet another herd on the rise. On seeing them, I hid behind the bough of a tree and fervently hoped that the elephants would have no reason to approach the cliff's edge. I looked down and saw that the elephant herd below me had scented my lions with their raised trunks. The elephants trumpeted, crashing forwards. I heard trees being smashed, screams and more trumpeting. The noise was so tremendous that I felt that it was possible that one of the lions had been trampled and grew anxious as the commotion continued.

Minutes later, I saw the elephants move as one out of the thicket, which was just as well as the elephants near me on the cliff top were moving towards where I was hidden. I quickly scampered down the cliff and began calling softly for the lions. I did not come across a trampled lion! Instead, and quite unexpectedly, I found an entire elephant tusk complete with its root nerve. I realised then that one of the elephants had somehow knocked its tusk from its jaw while pursuing the lions. As I was inspecting the large tusk, Furaha appeared and took possession of my find. She settled down to pull out and then eat the large nerve – it was glistening red and almost snake-like in appearance.

I left her and went to investigate how the tusk had been knocked out. I soon discovered that the elephant, during its charge, had rammed its tusk with great force into the fork of a mopane tree and on to a solid leadwood tree. This had dislodged the tusk from the elephant's jaw and it had fallen to the ground. It had been a clean extraction and the tusk had not been snapped. This was fortuitous for the elephant. If the tusk had snapped off high up, the sensitive root nerve could have been exposed causing excruciating pain.

69

I could not leave the tusk where it lay as it would be discovered by poachers. I had to hand it over to the government wildlife officials. However, by carrying the tusk back to camp, I was now in the predicament of being in the unlawful possession of ivory. Would the Wildlife Department rangers honestly believe my tale of the lions being responsible for the elephant losing its tusk?

As I entered camp with the tusk, Julie added to my disquiet by asking me straightaway whether I had had to shoot an elephant in self-defence. I told her the tale, but the story sounded strangely unconvincing even to me.

I asked Julie to take the tusk to the nearest rangers' camp some two hours' drive away while I returned to the site of the incident to mark the spot where it had all happened. I placed branches and leaves over the blood-spots to protect them from the wind, preserving the evidence as much as I could for the rangers' inevitable investigation.

The rangers arrived at our camp the next day. They, not surprisingly, had not entirely believed the story which Julie had recounted to them the day before. They repeatedly asked, 'But where is the other tusk?' At the same time, because I was a friend of theirs, they did not want to suspect me of wrongdoing. I showed the rangers the clear signs of where the elephant had dashed forward, the marks where the tusk had hit the trees and the blood-spoor left on the ground as the elephant had bled from the empty tusk socket.

When all was clarified, the rangers and I collectively let out relieved chuckles and laughed at what must be one of the strangest ways in which to find yourself in possession of ivory – and the most unbelievable!

C H A P T E R

6

Circles of Steel

As Batian and his two sisters reached the age of twenty months, they were killing fairly regularly for themselves and I provided them with only half the meat that they had required six months previously. They no longer needed to be kept in their enclosure at night except on rare occasions, becoming largely nocturnal as all wild lions are. They hunted more prolifically and their range increased dramatically.

One night around this time, I deliberately kept the lions in their enclosure as during the day I had found the fresh tracks of four other young lions in the vicinity of Tawana. That night, these youngsters – two males and two females – visited the camp. I awoke to hear Batian attempting to attack the intruders from behind the enclosure fence. He and his sisters showed absolutely no fear of the sub-adults. If anything, they appeared angered and frustrated at not being able to chase the bold youngsters away. This incident signified to me that the time had come for my lions to challenge any other young lions venturing into their range and to assert their territoriality. This was the last time that I kept my lions in the enclosure. They were now completely free.

The next morning, I opened the enclosure door for the last time and had mixed feelings as they walked out into their wild world. The transition had happened. Only in an emergency would they ever again have to stay inside at night.

I watched with interest as Batian headed towards 'his' marking trees. To Batian's indignation, these trees had been jetted upon by the sub-adults the night before. Quickly but thoroughly, Batian 'remarked' his trees and did so repeatedly that evening and the following morning. These activities again signified that he had a sense of ownership. Watching him, I was reassured that their rehabilitation had so far been successful. In a word, they felt that they 'belonged'.

Early in April, a direct confrontation took place between my lions and the four sub-adults. It happened one morning as I was following in the tracks of where my three had walked the night before. I was suddenly alerted by the sounds of loud hollow growls about a kilometre away. I began to run in the direction of the sounds, which was where my lions' tracks led. I came upon an open plain area and saw three young lions moving towards where I subsequently discovered Batian in conflict with a male a little older than himself. Then I saw Rafiki and Furaha moving towards these lions.

I soon found myself involved in the confrontation taking place. Almost unconsciously and prompted by a strong protective feeling, I acted to support my lions. It was, after all, four against three. I was merely levelling the numbers! I called to my lions, not as a human, but in the 'Ooweh' lion way I had learnt from my lions – the way they would call to each other. Rafiki and Furaha turned on hearing me, and saw me just as the sub-adults started to run towards them.

Batian then appeared from his fray in the thick bush, approaching me as Rafiki and Furaha rushed up. A brief greeting ceremony took place between us, the pride – not including me – regrouping before they turned to chase the wild lions. I too ran forward following my trio. The sub-adults fled as we chased them for about a kilometre and a half.

Once the sub-adults had been seen off, my lions greeted me in full and with much excitement before beginning to scent-mark and scrape, again demonstrating their sense of 'belonging'. That night and the following day, my lions remained in the vicinity of the confrontation, making a plain statement of territorial ownership. I was incredibly proud of my lions – George's lions – wild and free.

The four sub-adults were, incidentally, all part of the Lower Majale pride in the south, sons and daughters of the old veteran, Darky. Over the next few weeks I saw signs, read from tracks and evidence on the ground, that my lions had at least two more confrontations with the sub-adults and had acquitted themselves well enough to prompt the trespassers to return south.

Poaching, one of the great scourges of African wildlife, increased in the Tuli shortly after the time of these confrontations. One evening, furtively and unseen, a group of men crossed the reserve's eastern boundary – the wide, sweeping, though largely waterless Shashe river. Over the following evenings, other men entered the reserve and, having completed their secretive work, returned to Zimbabwe across the Shashe's sands. What each group of men had in common was poaching, and carried with them large numbers of wire snares which they cunningly set in the south-eastern portion of the reserve.

Once set, the snares were almost invisible and, at a glance, could be mistaken for vines or thin branches. They lay awaiting the heads and necks of animals on the game trails, in the thickets of acacia bush and in the dark depths of the rich riverine. Over the following days, animals were caught by the snares and choked to their deaths – a kudu, then another, a waterbuck, three impala. The poachers returned, setting up temporary camps where they first butchered their victims, hanging the meat to dry, then later carried their prizes back to Zimbabwe.

At night, the scavengers – jackal, hyena and inevitably lion – were lured into the area of poaching activity by the smell of flesh and the stench of decay and death. A dead lion caught in a snare set for game would present the poacher with a windfall. The skins can be smuggled into South Africa and sold for a handsome price. The body parts can be collected and sold to 'sangomas' (witchdoctors) to be used as powerful 'muti' (traditional medicine). The two males of the Lower Majale sub-adult group were amongst those meat-eaters attracted by the smells. In the darkness, they walked closer to the snares which had not been deliberately set for them, but for those that they too preyed upon. One of the sub-adults stopped abruptly, caught by a snare. He pulled backwards, feeling the pressure around his neck. Then he fought the wire, startling his brother who ran to one side and he too was caught by a nearby snare.

The lions strained and in a frenzy tore at the ground. Branches splintered and the tightness around their necks intensified. Suddenly one male broke loose, the snare snapping from where it had been tethered at the base of a tree. The male ran off grunting in shock as the wire loop persistently clung to his neck. The snare's tail, where it had broken, trailed in the dust as he ran. The second male later also broke loose and fled. The lions were fortunate to have been caught by single-strand wire snares. If they had been caught by the three-strand type – wires plaited together for extra strength – or thick cable snares, both lions would have perished.

Amazingly, over the next few days, the lions managed to rid themselves of the circles of wire around their necks and totally freed themselves. This rarely happens with snared lions, who usually have to be tranquillised before the snare can be released, a task I have taken part in with a veterinary friend of mine too many times in the past. The injury to the muscles of these two lions' necks must have been considerable, but both in time fully recovered. They were indeed the lucky ones.

However, the poaching in that area continued with more animals dying. No regular anti-poaching work was taking place within the entire Tuli reserve at that time. Some patrolling occurred, but it was spasmodic, inconsistent and therefore largely ineffective.

I received a radio call one day from Silius, a member of the Charter Reserve staff. As Bruce Petty, the warden, was away, he contacted me to tell me that some set snares had been found, snares that were just a small proportion of what actually existed. Over the next ten days, we recovered approximately two hundred and fifty snares. Five Zimbabwean poachers were caught and eight others were arrested by the local police, who came quickly to the reserve upon receiving a message about the extent of the poaching activity. We found the remains of four impala and a young kudu at a rough camp – a fraction of the real number of animals killed, butchered and carried back into Zimbabwe.

The poachers were not of the subsistence kind, but what can be described as 'meat merchants'. Two of the poachers caught told me how they sell a single stick of dried meat in Zimbabwe for two dollars. One snared kudu would reward them with at least four hundred dollars. With the low risk of being caught, it was a lucrative occupation. How many animals were lost during this time will never be known, but, once again, the situation illustrated how unprotected and vulnerable many areas of the reserve were.

It was during the time of this considerable poaching activity that an incident occurred that will always remain fresh in my mind. As Silius and I were searching for any snares we may have missed previously, an impala herd rushed ahead of us, bouncing and leaping with life in a blur of gold and white, a beautifully graceful sight. Suddenly I saw an impala struggling frantically on the ground behind the herd and felt sickened. The impala had been caught in a snare. Silius and I rushed forward and held the impala as still as possible as we managed to release the snare from around its back and soft white belly.

The snare was loosened and we stood back as the impala, in some shock, rose to its feet and then, panic-stricken, leapt away noisily. This was the eleventh-hour action, removing the snare just before it killed. I shook my head with frustration. The impala had been saved by us, but only because we happened to be there. I thought, 'How many others are dying weekly throughout the Tuli bushlands because of the chronic lack of any anti-poaching initiative?' Back at camp, I told Julie once again about the snaring I had seen in this area in the past (and of the slaughter of elephants by poachers with AK47s during the early 1980s). She nodded as I spoke and we concluded that protection for wildlife in the Tuli had not improved. Basic grass-root conservation was not being achieved. I remember saying to Julie in my anger that it was ironic that people could afford the luxury of owning private reserves and yet could not afford to protect the wildlife they wished to view or wished their tourists to view. Although I was indebted to many of the landowners for allowing me to bring the lions to the area, I could not help but feel angered by the fact that, despite years of such poaching pressure, the owners had still not collectively implemented full-time anti-poaching for the entire area. This in spite of my many written reports in the past urging the necessity for anti-poaching measures, and focusing upon the pressures facing the area's wildlife, particularly the Tuli lions.

Having been made aware once more of the extent of poaching activity, it was clear to me why the regional lion population had not risen in the years I had been away. In fact, it had declined. It was at this point of frustration that I wondered whether I should move my lions elsewhere. It was, in reality, a catch-22 situation. The lions' rehabilitation was going so well. I really did not want to retard their progress, but, I asked myself, 'What about the dangers that exist here? Where is the last Eden?' We decided that we would have to tackle the poaching problem ourselves.

Julie and I knew that, despite our limited resources, it was imperative to introduce and finance our own anti-poaching team, to be employed by the Tuli Lion Trust, our small conservation organisation. It took another four months before we had enough money to employ and train an anti-poaching team, a team that grew from two men to an eventual four. In the interim period, our initial sponsors, Tuli Safari Lodge, upon hearing of the situation, occasionally made a few members of staff available to assist me with patrolling, and some good work was achieved.

Also during this time we had in our employ a young man named Mafika Manyatsa, who assisted Julie with camp duties. Mafika did not really enjoy his somewhat isolated life at Tawana and so, after some discussion on the matter, we all decided that it would be far more constructive if he did patrolling work. He moved to one of the Charter Reserve camps and joined two staff members there whose duties included anti-poaching work. Mafika in time became the leader of the Tuli Lion Trust anti-poaching team.

So, at least until our own team was financed, some increased anti-poaching work took place, snares were removed and poachers occasionally caught. Additionally, I would spend hours patrolling alone in and around the lions' range, leaving behind hundreds of footprints which would signal to a poacher that this particular area was being well guarded. I suspect that on at least two occasions Zimbabwean poachers saw me while I was with the lions. Both times, while walking with the lions, I found fresh human footprints, and on one of these occasions, accompanied only by Rafiki, she became alert and skittish – signs that she knew someone was watching.

The story of my work with the lions had by this time been talked about in the neighbouring Zimbabwe villages. Not only would they, from their side, cross into the reserve, but staff members on our side would, just as illegally, cross the Shashe – some to visit family, others girlfriends, or at times to buy the potent Mlala wine, the alcoholic drink made from liquid tapped from Mlala palms.

Over the long months of seeing me patrolling along the river bank and because of the chatter that flowed across the Shashe, some Zimbabweans got to know me and I them. Meeting me at the centre of the Shashe, they would kindly give me news of any lions or elephants which had recently crossed the river into their lands or information on where they suspected poaching was occurring. This communication, the discussions about my work and my association with the lions had a beneficial effect, I believe. It was because of our presence that no new poaching began between the Pitsani and Tawana valleys where we lived – areas which previously were much favoured by Zimbabwean poachers.

The poachers' work was damaging, yes, though generally the people living adjacent to the reserve across the Shashe, the 'people of the Shashe' as I began to think of them, were people I admired. Those who lived upon the Shashe's banks were dependent upon this great, at times blinding, river of sand, for beneath the sand lay water for which they dug for their own requirements and the needs of their livestock. The river and the people were a paradox; the sand riverbed was wide, expansive and seemingly dry, but supported hundreds of people and hundreds of animals, domestic and wild. These people, many desperately poor, with their tired faces and tattered clothes were from a distance like shadows of melancholy. But when they were laughing with me or when the children splashed and played in the rain-revived river, they were the essence of the warm-hearted Africa I had grown up in.

Snaring is just one of the many threats to the Tuli lions and all the region's wildlife. Another threat was pending though – the legal hunting of lion.

It was official. Lion hunting was to take place in the neighbouring Tuli Safari Area (also known as the Tuli Circle) in Zimbabwe during the 1990 hunting season. As mentioned previously, no fence divides the two reserves, thus allowing all wildlife free movement between the Tuli reserve in Botswana and the adjoining Tuli Circle in Zimbabwe.

We were exasperated. Legal hunting would further reduce the numbers of lions in the Tuli and could possibly cause my own lions to be destroyed within our first year in the area. I was very angry when I realised that prior to my bringing the lions to the Tuli, it was known to some people connected with the area that lion hunting took place in the neighbouring reserve. I had not been informed of this when I was planning to rehabilitate the lions in the Tuli.

My first knowledge of the hunting occurred several weeks after we had arrived from Kenya. However, much earlier in the year, months before George Adamson's murder and the consequent situation of the cubs, I had heard it rumoured that lion hunting was taking place in the Tuli Safari Area. Although at that time I was not working within the reserve, I immediately started investigating the rumour to see if it was true and if so, I would work towards a banning of lion hunting. Through a friend, I received information from a senior official of Zimbabwe's Department of National Parks and Wildlife Management that *no* hunting was occurring. I breathed a sigh of relief, putting the possible problem out of my mind. If that reply had been in the affirmative, I would have submitted a report to Zimbabwe's Department of National Parks illustrating why such hunting would be yet another damaging pressure upon a historically and currently stressed lion population and structure – information I had compiled for *Cry For the Lions* three years previously.

Julie and I knew that we had to act quickly to stop the hunting of lions from taking place. One morning while resting with my lions in the bush, I composed a lengthy letter to the Deputy Director of Zimbabwe's Department of National Parks and Wildlife Management, Mr George Pangeti. In this letter I outlined not only my lions' story, and George's legacy, but the past and current situation, as I knew it, of the Tuli lions. I stressed that the lions of the Tuli Safari Area in Zimbabwe and those of the Tuli reserve in Botswana were a single population, with individuals using both areas as ranges overlapped the joint region. In addition, I listed the known endangering pressures on the lion population – the snaring, the illegal luring of lions into South Africa where they are shot, and other factors. These pressures could not be seen as affecting only lions from Botswana but the structure of a joint population.

In due course, I received welcome and much appreciated news from Mr Pangeti. A year's moratorium was to be placed upon lion hunting by his Department. I once again let out a sigh of relief. We had saved some lives and bought time, but I knew realistically that the moratorium alleviated, in the short term, just one additional pressure upon the Tuli lions. A long-term ban on lion hunting was needed to act in conjunction with other protective measures, such as area-wide efficient anti-poaching, and predator-proofing to be implemented on two of the reserve's boundaries. Only once these measures were achieved would the Tuli's lion population truly be given an opportunity to stabilise and in time find its own natural population levels.

Hunting on a seasonal basis in the Tuli Safari Area of a broad spectrum of species takes place as a form of utilisation of wildlife. No tourism infrastructure exists in the area which would provide an alternative form of 'utilisation'. Annually, the Zimbabwe Hunters' Association is allocated a quota of the species available to hunt on what is judged to be a sustainable basis, thereby not affecting the species' overall population. In turn, income is generated for the government.

We communicated with the Association before the moratorium expired, and for two years after the expiry of the moratorium the Zimbabwe Hunters' Association decided not to recommence lion hunting. Communication was the key. Such communication had clearly been lacking on the Botswana Tuli side in the past.

It was clear to me and to most people why lions should not be hunted. For the same reasons – although legally entitled to hunt lions – the members of the Zimbabwe Hunters' Association decided not to hunt them. The population was not stable and could certainly not justify sustainable hunting. I could not understand therefore why people with interests in the Tuli had not also risen to call for a ban on lion hunting. Old Darky, the tourists' lion, the old lion that had been viewed and photographed by thousands of visitors over many years, often roamed into the Tuli Circle and he could easily have been hunted and killed.

Tourists visiting Africa seek the lion and have a great desire to see the animal which symbolises the African wilderness. The desire converts into dollars and pounds for the tourist operator and for the country itself. However, here in the Tuli, apart from our efforts and the co-operation of Zimbabwe's Department of National Parks and Wildlife Management and the considerable support and assistance of the Zimbabwe Hunters' Association, little was being done to stop this tourist attraction, this resource, from being destroyed. It was ironic to hear at the time how, in other private and national parks in southern Africa, lions were being reintroduced. Tourists' demands caused landowners in other areas to realise that live lions were more valuable than gold.

The lack of concern about such conservation issues in much of the Tuli began to loom like a grey fog over us – and in the months ahead, as we drew attention to other conservation issues, we attracted criticism from and came into conflict with some of those who own land in the Tuli bushlands.

CHAPTER

7

Wild Callings

By June, my lions, then nearly two years old, were ranging over an area of some forty-five square kilometres. They would still regularly come to my camp in the evenings. At this stage of the rehabilitation, I would more often than not have meat at camp to give to the lions if their hunting had not been successful.

On one occasion the lions appeared at camp and for some reason I had no meat available. Feeling sorry for them and angry at myself, I went to sit with the lions to commiserate with them. Little did I know that in fact the lions were going to have full bellies that night, provided by a somewhat unexpected source.

At about eight o'clock, the lions and I suddenly heard the sounds of rushing footfalls coming from the streambed nearby. In a rather sinister fashion, the running sounds stopped abruptly. There was silence. Moments later the sounds began again, becoming louder as whatever was out there approached at speed. In the light of my torch, I saw a hyena as it flashed by. The lions by this time were excited and dashed out of the enclosure just as I heard the distinctive bellow of an impala in distress.

The hyenas (from their tracks the next morning, I discovered that there were three of them), hunting co-operatively as a pack, had seized the antelope. I heard my lions rushing towards the hyenas and a confrontation of growls and snarls broke out with my lions clearly surprising the pack. For several seconds there was again silence. Then I heard the impala bellow for the last time – now in the possession of my lions. As if to add to the already confusing situation, two of the hyenas then ran past near where I stood and began calling in their eerie whooping 'Oooo – whup' way. During the night, I occasionally heard sounds of my lions feeding and early the following morning they came to camp, drank water, then led me to the kill. All that remained of an adult male impala was the head and some vertebrae.

Just after this 'opportunistic kill', I saw for myself again how adept the lions were becoming at fending for themselves. One late afternoon I was attempting to locate the lions by following their tracks which seemed to be leading towards one of their favoured areas – a water-point in the Pitsani streambed.

On the camp road, just by my wooden sign proclaiming 'Tawana Camp – No entry without prior permission', I came across the lions. I saw that they all had some blood on their faces and presumed because they were not full-bellied that they had killed something quite small earlier on. At my appearance, they greeted me and then began to head towards the Pitsani streambed a kilometre or so away. Upon reaching the water-seep, they drank from the small pool and then, to my surprise, began heading back to the camp sign. Rafiki and Furaha led the way while Batian and I followed slowly behind.

When Batian and I reached the sign, to my astonishment I saw Rafiki and Furaha lying up to one side near the bodies of two male impala. Only the bellies of the impalas had been opened by the lions. I then realised that when I had first come across the lions they were resting up after having made a somewhat unusual 'double' kill. One of the impala must have been a territorial male which was in conflict with an intruder. In such situations, male impalas violently clash horns, the sound of which would have alerted the lions. During such fights, which normally only last several minutes, the impalas become oblivious to all around them and are vulnerable to predators. My lions had taken advantage of the situation, and swept forward, surprising and then killing both impalas.

As the sun touched the horizon, I left the lions to their feast and returned to camp, where I proudly told Julie of the lions' feat. The following morning I returned to where I had left the lions, but found only Batian. He was still feeding determinedly, despite a fully belly and despite little of the impalas remaining.

After some time, I left Batian and found Rafiki and Furaha at the Pitsani water-point. I sat with them and was later surprised and then amused to see both lionesses with their bulging bellies rise and attempt to hunt some passing zebra. They were not successful and soon returned to where I sat to sleep off their meal. After a while, Batian joined us having eventually left the frugal remains of the double kill to the darting jackals which had gathered.

I have long believed that an unspoken language, telepathy perhaps is a more accurate term, exists between lions. I felt its existence between the lions and myself, just as George Adamson had experienced it in his long life with lions. His pride, for example, after months away would uncannily appear at camp when he grew most concerned as to their whereabouts and safety.

During my time at Kora, I also saw how the lions would arrive when George most needed to be emotionally uplifted. Demonstrations of telepathy between man and lion were perhaps first witnessed by George with Elsa. It was displayed, for example, on an occasion when Joy was away for a time and George did not have a set date for her arrival. One day, however, Elsa stayed close to the road leading to where George lived and remained there for the whole day. To George's astonishment, later in the early evening, Joy arrived back in her vehicle. George recognised that Elsa had somehow anticipated Joy's return.

I discovered with my lions that this sense of perception developed between us. I realised that the lions knew if I had become ill, for example, and their behaviour changed at such times. During a period of six weeks, I was unwell on two occasions. I was initially ill with malaria-type symptoms, then later was greatly troubled by an abscess near my lower intestine. On both these occasions, the lions ceased roaming in their widening range and stayed close to camp. The lions would come to me early each morning, then reappear again early in the afternoons, staying in the enclosure till late. As I lay upon my stretcher, which Julie had positioned beside the camp fence, the lions would greet me through the wire and lie nearby. Once I was well again, the lions immediately reverted back to their normal movement patterns, hunting and exploring their range, visiting camp only in the evenings.

This was extraordinary behaviour but, as time passed, there were similar occurrences. The lions would rarely visit the camp if we were away (this I concluded by the lack of their spoor outside camp) but would soon reappear on my return. On some occasions, just after Julie and I trundled into camp after being away for some days, the lions would arrive. Again the spoor on the ground would indicate that these were their first visits to the camp during the duration of our absences.

Still to this day, the lions sometimes arrive at camp within minutes of my waking up in the mornings. The sounds of their lapping water from the drum which I provide heralds their arrival. As I write, this very morning was an example. The lions had been away from camp for five or six days and just as I stirred from my stretcher at dawn, I heard the familiar sound of water being lapped. After drinking, the greetings always begin.

Julie and I developed a form of sensing which the lions possess. This became evident when a series of coincidences occurred just too often. One morning (remembering that the lions generally, at that time, only visited the camp in the evenings) when I was miles from camp on an anti-poaching patrol, I for some reason called Julie on my portable radio to ask whether she had seen any sign of the lions at camp. She replied that as she had first heard me calling her, she had suddenly seen the lions approaching camp. In the months ahead and up to the present day, it is not uncommon for me to call Julie, without any knowledge of the lions' whereabouts, to ask about them and for her to reply, 'As you called, the lions arrived at camp.'

Julie developed an uncanny and inexplicable perception of whether the lions would come to the camp on a particular night or not. We only began to realise this in time. If I was worried about the lions, I would ask Julie whether she thought the lions would appear at camp. Her 'yes' or 'no' replies proved to be far more accurate than pure coincidence.

'Sensing' in another form – being able to sense the lions' different moods, knowing when they were troubled – was reasonably easy for me. Lions are social animals, like man, and their 'body language' is quite pronounced. As a result of this expressiveness, I could to an extent read their feelings.

Being constantly concerned about the dangers posed to the lions by poachers, I would always become uneasy if just one of the lions appeared at the camp, or if two arrived with one being absent. One day, Rafiki 'expressed' her feelings to me and 'indicated' what she wished me to do. At eight o'clock one evening, she appeared at camp alone. She rushed excitedly into the enclosure and, I sensed, was clearly upset. She moaned considerably more than normal as she rubbed herself repeatedly against me. I acted out my part in the greeting ceremony in full and attempted to calm her by talking in the soft way I do when the lions appear troubled.

'All right, all right,' I cooed in the tone which the lions use when affectionately greeting each other, my words sounding, I hoped, like a kind of combination of man's vocal communication and that of lions.

Later I offered Rafiki meat and while she ate, Julie and I discussed where Batian and Furaha might be and why Rafiki seemed so upset. I was particularly concerned as just a few days earlier, I, together with some helpers, had pulled up a number of poachers' snares from an area lying on the edge of the lions' range. The area was known notoriously as 'Poachers' Valley'.

I then decided to call the missing two. Cupping my hands I called, 'Come on, Batian. Come on, Furaha. Look! Come on.' Normally, if the lions were within earshot of my calls, they would respond by heading back to the camp – if they were not on a kill that is. Rafiki grunted and moaned each time I called. She then paced along the camp's fence, and so I went out through the gate to be with her. She ran up, greeted me again affectionately before turning to set off hurriedly in a north-easterly direction.

Of course I could not follow her as there was little moon, but to try and comfort her, I accompanied her for a short distance. She would repeatedly stop, allowing me to catch up, but upon reaching her she would dash forward in a hurry. It was quite clear to me that she wished me to follow. In the months ahead Rafiki, on different occasions, would use this routine to encourage me to follow her.

I knew though that night that the best I could do was to follow her the next morning at first light – that was if she waited. I went back into camp and later, to my astonishment, saw her come back into the enclosure and then lie down to rest, lying as close to my tent side of the enclosure as possible. When I awoke in the morning she was still in the enclosure – clearly she had waited for me. Hurriedly I dressed and before sunrise I had already waved goodbye to Julie and was following

Rafiki as she did her stop-start routine to encourage me after her.

She led me north-east and my worries about Batian and Furaha intensified as I realised we were heading straight towards Poachers' Valley. She led me north up out of the valley towards the Tuli Circle. When we reached the border of Botswana and Zimbabwe I had to stop. If I crossed the border I would be entering Zimbabwe illegally. Strangely, at that point, Rafiki did not cross either and lay up literally where the two countries join. Was it possible she could somehow sense that I could not continue onwards? Could she sense that this was the edge of my range?

Later I left Rafiki resting up and continued alone down again into Poachers' Valley to search for tracks of Batian and Furaha, but the only signs I found were several days old. I pondered as to where they could be and realised that they were most probably indeed in the Circle where Rafiki had been heading. I sat in some shade by a streambed, frustrated and worried by the situation, with all the worst images and fears flashing through my mind.

I returned to where I had left Rafiki only to find that she had disappeared. Her spoor showed that she had not crossed into the Circle but had turned back in the direction of the camp. In time I found her moaning forlornly as she walked. We then trudged together over the long distance to Tawana. We arrived back at camp at sunset and I was more than a little exhausted after covering some thirty kilometres during the day.

I sat on the ground in the enclosure next to Rafiki, who still moaned at times, and recounted the day's events to Julie. Thirty minutes later Rafiki and I heard a familiar grunt behind us. We both spun around as Batian and Furaha dashed into the enclosure. We all greeted and I realised they were both noticeably full. They had been on a kill.

The following day I found their tracks on the Tuli Circle border where they had crossed back into Botswana very near where Rafiki and I had stopped the day before. If I had been able to cross into the Tuli Circle with Rafiki perhaps the whole story would have unfolded, but her actions during this time, her expressiveness, had clearly let her feelings be known to me and at least I had been of some comfort to her. I did not dwell too much on this and, exhausted, collapsed on to my stretcher, happy that all three had not come into danger, were unharmed and were resting nearby as my eyes closed.

It was in May that I initially suspected that Batian was roaring for the first time – calling out that sound that is as much of the spirit of the African wilderness as the very land itself. However, it was only in July that I first had the incredible experience of being beside Batian as he thundered out these calls.

July was a milestone period for many reasons, not only because Batian, despite being only two years old, was territorially secure enough to call as an adult. His mane too was at last blossoming. In the previous months, I had thought that due to his lack of development of a mane, Batian would be a 'maneless' male. This is a rare phenomenon in lions, but has been reported in parts of Africa. I knew of one maneless male in the Tuli in 1985. Probably the most famous maneless lions were those destroyed by Colonel R. J. Patterson in Kenya after more than one hundred Indian workers had been killed by the lions during the establishment of the railway line linking Mombasa to Nairobi late in 1898.

The time of Batian's first calls was also a milestone period because, for the first time, both Rafiki and Furaha showed signs of coming into oestrus – the 'cubs' had come into their 'teens.

Returning to Batian's roaring, I must first explain how in fact a lion does roar. A lion pulls air deep into its lungs, tightens its abdomen compressing the air, then releases it through the vocal cords, delivering an immense sound that can be heard literally kilometres away. The roar begins as a loud moan and then intensifies in volume into a series of full bellows, after which grunts follow, almost as loud as the bellows.

To some of Africa's peoples, and certainly to me, the lion's roar translated means, 'WHO IS LORD OF THIS LAND? . . . Who is lord of this land? . . . I AM . . . I AM . . . I am . . . I am.'

One morning in July, as I walked with Batian and Rafiki up a streambed, Batian began calling. The sounds were tremendous and all that was around us, the rocky cliffs, the trees, the ground itself, seemed to reverberate with Batian's proclamations. At one stage Batian began to call as my hand lay where his budding mane tapered into a narrow tuft between his shoulders.

The sound and the occasion were all-consuming. I was in the midst of the lions' ancient world, amidst life that roamed Africa's great savannahs before my kind had adapted to walk upright. Batian's calls, with the three of us in the wilderness, depicted a paradoxical scene of man's long relationship with lions. Early man's relationship with these animals was one of mutually benefiting competition. As time passed though, and as it is largely today, this relationship became unbalanced, destructive, consisting of man's continued and unrelenting persecution of his past competitor. As Batian called, I thought of early man, our dual past and of the following words written by veteran zoologist George Schaller:

> Our dual past still haunts us. We hear a lion roar and the primate in us shivers. We see large herds of game and the predator in us is delighted.

Batian's calls that morning also symbolised to me the lions' complete return to their world, a world from which they had been removed by the actions of man. Yet, with their wild lion hearts unblemished, they had been able to rediscover their true home, domain and role in the wilds.

I loved being amongst the lions as they called. These moments would momentarily complete an indefinable portion of my soul. Then, as their calls ended, as the echoes drifted into nothingness, this spiritual feeling would diminish and the incompleteness return.

I also experienced lighter moments while watching Batian call on occasions. I remember once as Batian began to call, Rafiki began to stalk him, then leapt on to him – a scene that somewhat belittled his grand statement. I sometimes also noticed that when Batian called the noise was too much for even his ears and after each bellow he would shake his head and ears from side to side, the reverberation clearly causing him some discomfort.

As previously mentioned, it was at this time that I saw Batian's sisters were, for the first time, coming into oestrus. One morning Rafiki appeared at camp alone after splitting up from Furaha and her brother. I noticed she seemed even more demonstrative towards me than usual, but not in the way I'd seen before when she wished me to follow her. She stayed right at camp throughout the day, anxious for my attention. Julie noticed that twice during the day when I had to leave on errands Rafiki would call persistently in loud moans in my absence. On my return she would immediately become possessive of me. Her behaviour puzzled me initially before I realised that her actions were prompted by her coming into oestrus.

In time, as she continued to mature, when she was on heat her behaviour became more elaborate and intense. She would present herself to me, pushing her hindquarters on to my legs, growling ominously with flattened ears, expressing that she wished to make love, not war! Still to this day I find myself in an awkward situation whenever Rafiki comes into oestrus.

A friend recently commented to me on this subject. 'Surely by now she realises that it's a waste of time to approach you when she's on heat, with you consistently being a hopeless potential mate.'

But always when coming into oestrus Rafiki splits up from Furaha to first seek me before eventually wandering across her range in search of a male lion. On occasions, apart from presenting herself to me, she jets copious amounts of urine up on to my chest or sometimes calmly urinates in a steady flow on to one of my legs and shoes. It is indeed a curious situation I have to go through at these times.

George told me once how he too at times would be caught in such awkward situations. He recounted how, 'several years ago' (when he was in his seventies) one particularly promiscuous lioness caused him to have to take drastic action because of her demonstrative overtures. The old man had to climb a nearby tree to escape her attentions and had to stay up there half a day until she finally wandered away.

It was in part due to the combination of Batian's calls and his sisters' early heats that one morning in July unwelcome company arrived at our camp. Julie and I were sleeping outside the tents, close to the camp fence, when Batian once again began his pre-dawn proclamations. We awoke to the sounds and then, in the twilight, twenty paces away, saw lions passing by. As I counted three, I at first presumed that they were my lions – until a fourth followed. Sitting upright, blinking sleep from our eyes, we then realised that two of the four were young males like Batian. It was the sub-adults whom I hadn't seen for many weeks. Loud calls then broke out from the north in the Tuli Circle, which I presumed were the two young males I was, at that time, beginning to know and whom I later named the Zimmales. As their calls tapered off I heard a lion call from the south. 'Old Darky responding,' I thought.

We counted up, as we watched the sub-adults sniffing at Batian's bushes, how many lions, by sight and hearing, we estimated were in the Tawana and Pitsani valleys. Including my lions there were ten lions around, members of three different prides. Never before nor since have we had such a number or diversity of lions in the vicinity of Tawana. After a while, as the sun rose, the sub-adults drifted away, the calling from the north and south stopped and I wondered where my lions were.

An hour later, with the sun risen and bright, I ventured out of the camp to look for the spoor of my lions. I found their spoor and followed, thinking that they would have headed away to lessen the chances of coming into confrontation with any of the array of other lions in the area. Their spoor headed towards a rise in the east. As I approached this area I was startled as a lion blasted a series of demonstration growls at me. Silhouetted against the bright light in the east I saw Darky, irate and advancing ominously. I shouted at him, expecting him to move back allowing me too to slowly withdraw. The opposite occurred. He continued to come forward, growling. I shouted again and in turn he bellowed an insult, but stopped momentarily.

I moved slowly backwards trying to get out of his view in the tangle of mopane trees, but found myself being followed as once again I had to shout at him and, in turn, he again bellowed his anger at me. 'He's going to follow me right to camp if this keeps up – or worse,' I muttered to myself.

I was also thinking that soon I would have to fire a warning shot into the air with the rifle I was carrying. Fortunately, I did not have to resort to this. After one more 'shout-bellow' session, Darky allowed me to back away, getting out of his view, and I was soon heading back to camp. I must admit that even when I was quite close to camp I still repeatedly turned around, half-expecting old Darky to be following in the shadows. Indeed it was unusual behaviour which he displayed and the first time I had been followed by him in all the time I had known the old lion.

Later that same morning, conflict was occurring in the south. Darky had headed back into his Lower Majale territory and I was informed by my ranger friend, David Marupane, as I drove south, that he had seen Darky being rushed at by the sub-adults and in turn Darky repeatedly attempting to follow them. All this was happening some distance from Tawana and well within the Lower Majale area.

I subsequently found the sub-adults and Darky, and after watching the situation I felt that perhaps one or both of the young lionesses might have been on heat, attracting the veteran who was at the same time being deterred from approaching the lionesses by their brothers, his sons.

Darky, once Batian began calling regularly, rarely came to Tawana after this time. It is one of his last visits that shall always remain in my mind.

One morning I awoke to rustling sounds at 'Batian's bush' – Batian's favourite mopane tree, next to the fence, which he would regularly scent into and scrape below. My lions had been near the camp the night before and, upon seeing a portion of tawny head in the leaves and branches, I got up from the stretcher and, stark-naked, walked forward calling, 'Batian . . . Batian.'

When I was within a pace from the fence dividing me from the tree, a huge head and mass of dense black mane appeared from around the tree – Darky! At the same time, I heard a little voice behind me in the tent saying nervously, 'I don't think it's the cubs, Gareth.'

I do not know which of us got the greater shock – Darky or I. I yelled at him, taking a jump backwards as he too leapt aside and loped off, uttering a series of indignant grunts. Darky was, unbeknownst to me, in the process of scenting on Batian's bush when he was startled by my appearance. Julie had watched this whole scenario and now, very much awake, hooted with laughter as, back in the tent, embarrassed by what had occurred, I began pulling on my shorts. One feels more naked than naked when confronting a fully grown male lion just a yard away!

CHAPTER

8

Tooth and Claw, Hoof and Horn

By July, Rafiki and Furaha were both regularly coming into oestrus, each time wandering north in search of males and often finding them. Lionesses seem to reach sexual maturity at least six months earlier than the males. Therefore, with both lionesses somehow recognising Batian as an unsuitable mate, they sought adult males.

Furaha, initially more so than Rafiki, would spend days away from the pride's normal haunts, consorting with one or the other of the Zimmales – the two young males, probably brothers, who resided in the southern Tuli Circle. After the period of mating, she would reappear at Tawana, scratched on her neck and hindquarters from the typically demonstrative lion courtship, and smelling strongly of having been in the company of a male. Her reappearance would create excitement in Batian and Rafiki who, if in the area, would examine her and smell her persistently – so much so that she would constantly have to skip away, uttering short growls in an attempt to escape their questioning noses.

On these occasions, her reaction towards me was always that of affection. At times, she would sit as close as possible to me and try and escape Batian and Rafiki's unyielding curious scrutiny. Always at this time, I too scrutinised the lionesses, feeling for any sign of pregnancy. Whenever Rafiki and Furaha sought the Zimmales, Julie and I would speak about how the incredible time would soon arrive when the 'cubs' would have cubs.

Unfortunately, this exciting period was to be overshadowed. A problem was escalating that posed yet another direct threat to my lions and other lions in the Tuli – the cattle issue along the Shashe. For many years, as each winter progressed, Zimbabwean livestock – cows, goats and sheep – would begin in increasing numbers to cross the great sand expanse of the Shashe and enter the Tuli to graze. The people of the Shashe had, through the sheer numbers of their livestock, combined with the fragility of the arid area, overgrazed their communal lands. The land could not support the great herds and so each year the herders would drive the beasts illegally across the riverbed to graze in another country, Botswana, in an area set aside for wildlife, the Tuli.

In recent years, the landowners and managers of the Tuli have been plagued by the perennial problem, and each year no permanent solution could be found. A respite from the cattle pressure and associated problems would occur with the coming of the rains. As the Shashe's waters rose, the livestock herds would then be driven back to Zimbabwe where they would stay for a few short months. The problem would be forgotten until the following year as winter approached, when, as ritually as a sunrise, the cycle would recommence.

The effects of hundreds of head of livestock year after year being illegally grazed in the reserve was severe. Firstly, valuable winter feed for the grazing wild species would be consumed by the livestock. Conflict would arise as lion, leopard and hyena would prey upon the ample herds. When a cow was killed by lions, the livestock herder, incensed by his loss, would drive away the pride and set many snares around the carcass of the beast, anticipating the lions' return. The lions would go back to their kill and in turn could be caught in the snares to die a terrible death.

Over the years, the effects of cattle/predator conflict reduced the original pride structures along the Shashe almost to non-existence. 'An eye for an eye, a tooth for a tooth' – this, the livestock-owners' code, was in reality a cycle of conflict resulting in an all-lose situation. Cattle were killed, lions were killed, and as long as just a handful of lions existed in the Shashe – those killed in turn being replaced by others lured to the area by easy prey – and as long as the cattle herds grazed in the reserve, the cycle of conflict would and did continue.

During the winter of 1990, as my lions, now almost independent of me, explored further afield, the cattle problem intensified. Poachers, ever opportunistic, would take advantage of the situation, venturing into the reserve under the guise of herders. They placed snares for the wildlife, but their activities angered the herders as cattle were also commonly caught and killed by the snares.

I remember one morning being called up on the radio by Mafika (our ex-camp assistant, now a member of the Charter Reserve staff on anti-poaching work). He informed me that he had discovered fifteen snares near the Shashe river, two of which held cows; one dead, one alive. I drove quickly to the area and there, with the staff, inspected the grisly scene. The live cow was fortunate in being caught on its leg by the wire and we released it. The other, a pregnant cow, lay dead and grotesquely bloated. The snare was tight around its neck and had strangled the animal to death. I saw how, when the cow was first caught, it had run in desperate circles, wrapping the length of wire round and round the tree to which the snare was attached, until she had found herself bound hard against the tree's trunk. As the cow had slowly died, she had begun to abort the life within her. The cow had died just as her calf's head had emerged and there the calf too had died – died while being born.

Because of the abundant prey in the form of livestock, coupled with the fact that the Shashe area was not held territorially by a single pride, the other lions of the Tuli began utilising this area, in a sense attracted to the danger zone. As winter progressed, more cattle were killed. My lions too ventured east to the topmost section of the Sashe. As a result of this and my fears for their safety, I spent much of my time locating the lions. If I found them towards the east, I would call them loudly from the hills in the evening, encouraging them to the safer area of the Tawana and Pitsani valleys.

The inevitable day occurred when I discovered that my lions had killed a cow near the Shashe. My lions had been driven off the cow by three Zimbabwean herders. I was in the area with Mafika and other staff, and came across and then caught the herders who were hacking up the carcass and were about to take some of the meat back to their village. We discovered the men just in time for they could have placed snares around the cow's remains to avenge its death – and my lions could have returned to the carcass . . .

I questioned the Zimbabweans about what had happened. Freely, they told me that from their village beyond the river, they had seen vultures circling on our side, signalling a death. They crossed the Shashe to investigate and discovered three lions, a young male and two females, feeding on one of their cows. The Zimbabweans then shouted at the lions, who fled at the appearance of the men. They then began butchering the cow and that was when they were discovered by us. We took the men to the borderpost, Pont Drift, and handed them over to the immigration officials.

We returned to the Shashe to search for my lions and found them resting two kilometres away from the cow's carcass. By this time, it was four thirty in the afternoon and I planned to lead them out of the dangerous areas of cattle and poaching activity before nightfall when normally they would become active again.

I told Mafika to leave me where I was and drive the vehicle away, and to inform Julie that I would try and walk my lions the fourteen kilometres back to Tawana before sunset. As the vehicle left, I called to the lions, who slumbered some five hundred metres away. They appeared from the bush and trotted forward to greet me, no doubt a little surprised to see me. With our greetings complete, I began walking west, calling them. They, with their unquestioning trust, followed and we trudged onwards as the sun lowered. At intervals along our way, I found several snares which I angrily pulled down.

Later, when the sun was reduced to a red ball upon the horizon, I knew that I now had to run if I was to arrive at camp before it was completely dark. I jogged, stopping at intervals to call the lions, who were now well out of the Shashe valley. I arrived at camp in virtual darkness and it was a most relieved Julie who met me at the gate. Mafika had informed her of the situation and she had waited for me, becoming increasingly anxious as the sun set. We then waited for the lions' arrival. Only ten minutes after my return, they appeared – tired, thirsty, but safe again.

The following day, over twenty poachers' snares were found in the general vicinity of where my lions had killed the cow, snares which, in Mafika's estimation, had been set two days earlier. My lions' unquestioning trust in me had protected them, but the other lions had no one constantly looking after them in that area where grave dangers lay.

Two weeks later, a Tuli lioness was caught by the poachers' wires. One snare clasped her neck, another her paw. She was one of the Lower Majale lionesses, lured to the Shashe by the concentrations of cattle. Somehow, unimaginably, she broke both the snares, but in her fight was badly injured. She then hobbled south-west towards the Lower Majale, many kilometres away.

She was reported to have been sighted and searched for, but without success. I was hampered in my search by not having been granted traversing rights on certain private reserves in the Tuli. Approximately a week after she was snared, I was told that the lioness had been seen on a portion of the Tuli used for tourism. I was also informed that the management of that private reserve had 'been too busy with tourists' at their camp to dart and treat the lioness! On hearing this, I was exasperated. It again highlighted to me the strange attitude which prevails towards wildlife in the Tuli in certain quarters.

Eventually, however, the lioness was thankfully darted and treated. I heard that the snare on her leg had wrapped tightly around her paw, like a high-tension coiled spring, and was a hideous sight. The pain and suffering she had endured must have been almost unbearable.

The Shashe cattle herds would in the evenings move out of the Tuli across the riverbed to the cattle-posts. In turn, lions would cross too, hunting at their typical time in darkness. Villages thus began to lose cattle on the Zimbabwean side at night, a situation ignited originally by their grazing of livestock in the Tuli. As some cattle were killed close to villages, the people of the Shashe understandably complained to the local Zimbabwean authorities. In the middle of August, it was reported from Zimbabwe that any lion found outside the Tuli and in the Shashe communal areas would be shot to curb the cattle killing. Fortunately, the person assigned to shoot lions did not act immediately for fear that an Adamson lion might be killed. To our immense gratitude, this person contacted us about the situation, and gave us time to act.

When I heard this alarming news, I first contacted George

Pangeti of Zimbabwe's Department of National Parks and Wildlife Management to state my perception of the problem and also state the lions' case. I was referred to the regional warden of that portion of Zimbabwe, and during my conversation with him, he agreed that no lions would be shot for the meantime, allowing us some time to seek a solution to the conflict.

Over the next few weeks, we held meetings with different authorities and pleaded with the relevant Botswana government departments to act upon the root of the issue – the cows being herded across the Shashe to illegally graze in the Tuli reserve. We also looked at the situation in a broader context. We proposed that the people of the Shashe be consulted about the idea of creating a wildlife buffer zone in the region where the people presently lived. This long-term project would involve pumping water for the people and livestock from the Shashe to an area thirty kilometres inland which was once the people's traditional grazing area. The lack of water had caused them to leave this area which was why they had settled along the Shashe river. We strove towards the fulfilment of this project with other conservationists, a project which would benefit both wildlife and people as well as curb the cattle/predator conflict. However, that was a long way off, and an immediate short-term solution needed to be found.

In the hope of alleviating the conflict, I arranged a meeting between representatives of the Tuli landowners, the Botswana police, wildlife department, immigration department, veterinary department and representatives of the Shashe livestock owners, wildlife officers and a local chief. This meeting took place on the Shashe and a long discussion ensued as ironically cattle drifted past us, crossing to and from Botswana. Our Botswana delegation was headed by my good friend Bane Sesa, Chief Immigration Officer for the Tuli area. He was greatly concerned about the problem, not only from a conservationist viewpoint, but also because, due to the cattle situation, Zimbabweans were constantly entering and leaving Botswana illegally.

The meeting concluded with the Zimbabweans being asked to first remove and then keep their cattle out of the reserve. They admitted that they knew they were doing wrong, but obviously wished their herds to prosper. The Zimbabweans present did, however, express interest in the long-term water project in their traditional grazing area and we promised to continue working on this very involved proposal.

The talks were a partial success. Cattle were removed and the numbers of livestock grazing in the Tuli were much reduced for some time. We continued to seek a more effective short-term solution, assisted by the Botswana authorities, and, a year and a half later, the problem was virtually under control.

In the interim, however, there were tense times. The Zimbabwe authorities stated again that lions would be shot and we again stated the lions' case. I resorted at this time to putting white identification collars on my lions and informed the person instructed to shoot lions following cattle across the Shashe that my lions now had identification. I also said that I would pay compensation if it was proved conclusively that my lions had killed cattle in the communal areas. No claims were ever made.

Many more times, I had to lead my lions away from the Shashe. Every time they headed eastwards, my blood would chill with anxiety and fear. Fortunately, no shooting of lions occurred. This was partly because of the reduced number of cattle grazing in the Tuli, resulting in fewer lions following the herds into the communal lands, and partly because our acquaintance in Zimbabwe was reluctant to shoot lions, even though he had government approval to do so. The lions' survival was in no small way due to his sympathetic attitude.

The presence of the Adamson lions in the Tuli, as in the case of the legal hunting of lion, had prevented other lions being destroyed. Being the focus of so much public attention, my lions had highlighted a major threat to predators of the Tuli and, in turn, their lives and those of other lions were less endangered as a result of the positive actions taken. This was another reminder of the major conservation benefits which my lions' presence had brought to the Tuli.

Early in October 1990, as our first anniversary in the Tuli with the lions approached, temperatures began to soar. The typically oppressive summer and promises of rain had begun. The Tuli truly is a land of contrast, a land of stark arid beauty for most of the year, but also for a few short months during the rains, suddenly alive with water, new leaves and blossoming flowers. The rain was always unpredictable. I will, though, always remember how, in the summer of 1990, we had our heaviest downpour of rain at Tawana –

a total of 96 millimetres which fell in less than an hour, this amount of rain representing almost one-third of an average total annual rainfall in the Tuli.

The downpour occurred during the night of the day on which Julie had returned from a few days away in Johannesburg. I had met Julie at Pont Drift in the late afternoon, and on the journey north to Tawana, we gazed at the thunderheads building up, rising almost like floating impenetrable fortresses in the skies. Upon reaching the camp and unloading, we heard the grumblings of the storm. Living in such a dry area, we had learnt that thunder and the approach of dark cloud did not necessarily mean that rain would in fact fall. The releasing of the desperately needed lifeblood from the sky is a fickle thing here. Often a storm might approach, wind would whip around furiously, then subside, as lightning crackled. Then we would hear and see the patter of rain and our excitement would often be uncontrollable – but quietness would come, the clouds move elsewhere, the sky clear and we would be left feeling greatly let down.

That evening, however, Julie and I could never have imagined, nor have we experienced again, the downpour we were to receive. The wind built up and we rushed around as usual packing entire bookshelves loaded with books and files into waterproof plastic bags and tightening the guy-ropes of the tents. Drops of rain began to fall as we finished our pre-storm chores and we bundled into our tent. As the sounds of the storm encircled us, we lay on the stretchers in our three-by-two-and-a-half-metre tent, chatting excitedly. As we talked, we heard the rain beginning to fall harder and eventually, to this sound, we both fell asleep.

Julie awoke, though, sometime later and hearing the intensity of the rain, left me sleeping to go out and check on the situation in the camp. The next thing I knew was the tent zip being opened and I heard Julie calling to me urgently. In the light of her torch, we saw to our amazement that suddenly water was flowing in torrents right through the tent. It was over a foot deep! My shoes were swirling against the tent's side as was a plastic cup, a magazine and the drenched remnants of a paperback book. It was like having a tent pitched in the middle of a stream. I then heard Julie shout, 'Gareth, the stream has risen way over its banks. Water's pouring through the kitchen area and rising by the jeep!' Now wide awake,

I quickly retrieved my shoes from the water, put them on, and, with Julie, splashed out towards the kitchen. Water, streaming from the sky, rushing along the ground, was everywhere. As I reached the kitchen, I saw the rush of water where the jeep stood. The water swirled just beneath its low engine and I feared it was about to be flooded. I called to Julie above the sound of the rain, saying we would have to get the jeep on to higher ground. I tried the jeep's starter, but it failed to fire. We then pushed the jeep, shoving and straining, but we were pushing against a slope and kept on slipping in the mud and water. By now, Julie and I were not only completely wet and mud-splattered, but also chilled to the bone. In desperation, I tried the starter again, then again and just when I thought that the engine had been completely flooded, the jeep started with an angry growl. I shot into the driver's seat and reversed the jeep out of the water and over the slope to higher ground where although the water was flowing, it was much more shallow.

I parked, then tripped back to where I had left Julie. I found her crouched in the water, pointing her torch left and right with her one hand while with the other she was grabbing at objects – she was attempting to retrieve some of our kitchen utensils, plates and cups, which were racing away with the waters.

Later we trudged up to the rainfall gauge and were aghast when we read how much rain had fallen. The rain then began to slow in its intensity and we headed back to our tent, and surrounded by now at last subsiding water, we eventually fell asleep again.

We awoke in the morning to sweet bird calls, their songs seemingly clarified to perfection by the dustless air cleansed by rain. The sun shone brightly and the sky was completely clear. Our tent, though, was a mess. Mud lay like brown sludge across the groundsheet and, to my astonishment, I saw the dark 'tide mark' where the flooding waters had pushed up against the tent on the outside. The water had banked up to about half a metre high the night before. We stepped out of the tent and set about picking up and finding what we could of our strewn belongings. I then went outside camp to walk or rather slip along the stream bank, and at intervals I would find bottles, cups and other things from camp, including one of my shoes (the other I only found weeks later, much further downstream). We spent the entire day sorting out the camp after that downpour, which illustrated once again how the Tuli is a land of extremes.

During the mid-summer of that year, the Pitsani river held long pools and clear waters that slipped slowly southwards down to the Limpopo. On particularly beating hot days, when the temperatures in the shade were touching the high forties, Julie and I would head off to the Pitsani. There, in the shade of a huge Mashatu tree overhanging the little river, we would undress, then experience almost painful luxuriance as we stepped into the river, the water tingling and stinging our hot skin. As we enjoyed the waters, we would, sitting or lying together, watch for other occupants of the pool – such as the terrapins with their algae-covered hard shells. On our appearance, the sun-basking terrapins would be disturbed and dive into the water. There they would remain for a long time before rising to the surface to breathe, then dive again. Terrapins are mainly carnivores which prey upon others of the water, such as insects, frogs, tadpoles and any carrion they might find. Julie has an inherent curiosity and interest in all forms of life, but I had long ago warned her not to be over-curious of, or try to handle, terrapins. By means of scent glands, these creatures can emit a mind-shaking odour which acts as one of their protective measures. This smell lingers on fingers and hands for long periods, despite frequent washing. Incidentally, the smell is not dissimilar to the pungent scent left by a male lion after he has jetted on to a bush, but is very much stronger. I have heard that the terrapin's scent frightens horses and donkeys who apparently mistake it for that of lion.

With the skin of our fingers and feet creased by prolonged submergence in the water, we would rise and then for some minutes, simply stand in the shade to become even cooler, eking out as much coolness as possible before having to inevitably step back into our clothes and then get into the searing heat of our vehicle to drive back to our baking camp.

Furaha and Rafiki were by this time largely independent of me in terms of fending for themselves. This was reflected when, on their sojourns north into the Zimmales' domain, they would return a week or more later looking fit, having hunted well for themselves and often with full bellies. When coming into oestrus, both lionesses would normally head north towards the perennial spring just inside the Tuli Safari Area known as New England, the focal point of the Zimmales' range.

I do not know who gave this spring such an unlikely name, although I have heard that it was the pioneers in the late 1890s, trekking north into what became Rhodesia, who referred to the waters as 'New England'. Indeed the spring must have been a welcome sight to these travellers, for here reliable waters bubble up into a series of pools beneath an ancient fig tree, a place where two nearby trees offer circles of shade – a rare oasis in a harsh, hot land.

The era of the pioneers has now long passed. Today, New England persists in providing much to the age-old original inhabitants of the Tuli – the wildlife. From miles around the oasis, game trails – those time-worn paths etched upon the red earth by thousands of animals' hooves, pads and toes – lead towards this area like the spokes of a wheel. This was clearly the reason for the Zimmales centring their range around New England, and for the lions the spring is also a place of plenty, a rich killing ground. Antelope head from afar to the waters to quench their thirsts, and some do not leave; they die here, enabling lions and others to live on.

When Batian attempted to follow his sisters north, confrontations between him and the Zimmales would take place at or in the vicinity of New England. After the initial conflicts, Batian, forlorn and deeply scratched and bleeding, would head south-east back to me at Tawana. He would appear at camp, or I would find him on his way, with flanks streaked with long gashes, his lower legs patchy with his own tar-like faeces. Like leopards, lions too will defecate when in a vicious confrontation with others of their kind. My heart would go out to Batian, always the loser in these initial confrontations, fighting one or other of the Zimmales whom, I estimated, were six to eight months older than him and that much larger. After such fights, I would spend hours with Batian, knowing that he saw me as a source of comfort and support and also as a fellow pride male. Despite his initial defeats, Batian's courage would never diminish. After being back in his domain for a few days, he would, often accompanied by me, call loudly to the north, in the direction of where his sisters were consorting with the Zimmales.

In time, as Batian grew and more battles were fought, the Zimmales began to respect Batian's 'ownership' and rarely entered his core area – the region of the Tawana and Pitsani valleys. It is also important to remember that Batian was not alone in his territorial claim. His proclamations would be supported by both his sisters. It was only when they were in oestrus that the lionesses would seek out the Zimmales. When not in oestrus, they showed no indication of associating with them. Rather, a contrasting attitude of antagonism and territoriality prevailed.

Sometimes confrontations would take place between my lions and the Zimmales which I would be involved in at Tawana when the lions, including the Zimmales, were still fairly young. One early morning, Julie and I awoke to the sounds of lions fighting. Still at camp at this time was Mafika, our camp assistant. I went outside through the camp gate to investigate the situation, leaving Julie heading towards our small kitchen area where Mafika was cleaning dishes. The two of them were unknowingly soon to be in the midst of a confrontation near the kitchen between my lions and the Zimmales.

Minutes after stepping out of camp, I spied Rafiki trotting towards me, followed by Furaha and then Batian. All three lions were highly excited. They greeted me and scent-marked vigorously and I noticed that all three had superficial scratches on their bodies, though no real damage had been inflicted during the initial confrontation.

'Where are the Zimmales?' I wondered. 'Are they watching?'

My lions and I turned as one when we heard a muffled grunt from a low, small hill a short distance from the kitchen side of the camp. My lions then, literally as a charging pack, rushed towards where the sound had come from, and I followed. As I ran, I heard the two groups of lions ahead of me coming into contact, followed by loud sounds of running lions rapidly approaching me. I tried to see who was advancing, but was momentarily blinded by the bright morning sun. I did, however, make out the forms of three lions as they flashed past close to me.

At the kitchen, Julie and Mafika, with plates and dishcloths in their hands, suddenly saw Batian streak past them in pursuit of one Zimmale, then the dashing forms of the other lions. Moments later, the other Zimmale came rushing past them; this time Batian was being chased with Furaha and Rafiki following behind his pursuer. Mafika and Julie watched all this to the accompaniment of me, just out of view, calling my lions, tramping around after losing sight of them earlier in the mêlée.

Soon, however, the confrontation ended. The Zimmales moved

back north, I came back into the camp and after we had discussed what we had all seen, Julie and Mafika resumed their activities in the kitchen. It was a somewhat tense start to the day's domestic chores!

Some months later, another confrontation with the Zimmales occurred at camp. One night, while Julie and I were peacefully reading in our tent, we were surprised by the loud sounds of lions in conflict – the furore seeming to come from the gate side of the camp. I rushed past Mafika's tent, which was pitched near the gate, and from his tent I heard not a sound. Mafika was either an extremely deep sleeper, not waking to the lions' tumultuous snarling sounds just fifteen to twenty metres away, or he was, with discretion being the better part of valour, simply keeping a low profile!

With torch and rifle in my hands, I went outside the camp as Batian and his sisters approached me. As I stepped forward towards them, I heard a hideously chilling growl to my right. I shone the torch and glimpsed the Zimmales with their then still short, scruffy manes moving back behind a small rise, but their growls still persisted. Determined to back up my pride and paticularly to demonstrate the much needed 'fellow pride male' support for Batian, I shouted loudly at the Zimmales. Their growls continued ominously and so I resorted to letting off a shot into the air. At this, the Zimmales dashed away, my lions rushed after them, conflict broke out and then all was quiet. Soon my lions reappeared, now having seen the trespassers off and bounded back to where I stood. In celebratory delight, they rubbed their bodies and heads against me as I in turn stroked and patted them.

Julie, however, I soon discovered, was not in such a delighted state. From her camp-bed, she heard me going out of the gate, then heard the growls, my shouts, the shot followed by the sounds of the short sharp final confrontation – then silence. She grabbed her torch, flung herself out of the tent and, wearing nothing much at all, scampered, as I had, past Mafika's still silent tent towards the gate. She approached the gate just as I was quietly letting myself into camp. At the sound of her approach, I shone my torch and saw Julie staring wide-eyed in her scantily clad state. I admit that I chuckled upon seeing her disposition, then told her that all was well at which she then trotted back again to the tent.

Silence still prevailed from Mafika's tent. I walked over and called his name, wanting to outline to him what was going on. 'Mafika,' I called. From somewhere in the depths of the tent, I heard him muttering drowsily (feigning sleep rather unsuccessfully, I thought). Then his head appeared from the flap and there, groggily wiping his eyes, he claimed that he hadn't heard a thing – not the lions, my shouts, the shot, nor Julie scampering past his tent. Disbelieving this, I bade him goodnight. Walking away, I thought that no one but a comatose person could have slept through all the commotion. Mafika's obvious code of 'discretion being the better part of valour' had prevailed, I think.

The rest of the night was uneventful. The Zimmales, I discovered in the morning, had taken off in one direction, and my lions had moved off to hunt, killing an impala that night down in the valley.

CHAPTER

9

Hunters and the Hunted

Putting identification collars on the lions due to the cattle conflict had further benefits. Furaha's collar had a radio tracking device, thus enabling me to locate and monitor the lions more easily and quickly. With radio tracking, my knowledge of their movements and kills increased enormously. Radio tracking also enabled me in time to determine that my lions' range was an area of one hundred and fifty square kilometres, an average-sized range for Tuli prides. Additionally, I discovered that the lions were killing a greater number of prey than I had initially thought, often killing far more than would be considered sufficient to meet their needs. I attributed this to the fact that certain of their prey species, such as kudu, were in poor condition and therefore more susceptible to predation by my young pride. They did not necessarily feed extensively on these out-of-condition animals. I also discovered that in fact they were killing a diversity of prey of varying condition.

In one five-day period while radio tracking the lions, I observed that they preyed upon one adult female kudu, one adult female eland, one warthog, one adult bull eland – and one large Zimbabwean ox that had for some weeks unwisely taken up residence in a valley in the eastern portion of my lions' range.

It was just after this period that I discovered that Furaha hunting alone had pulled down a huge eland bull. She was only twenty-nine months old at the time and would have weighed approximately 90–100 kilograms. Eland are the largest of the African antelope, and the bull killed by Furaha was in good condition; it would have weighed between 700–800 kilograms and was some 1.7 metres at the shoulder. I discovered her and her giant kill while radio tracking east of camp one morning. From my receiver, I got a strong signal from the lip of a small valley. There I found Furaha lying on the ground, panting, a few metres away from the eland. She had killed the eland just prior to my arrival. As I approached, Furaha rose wearily, greeted me and then slumped again to the ground, clearly exhausted from a long battle with the eland. She showed absolutely no aggression as I approached her kill. From the signs on the ground and marks on the eland itself, I was able to deduce how Furaha had killed an animal some seven to eight times her own weight. She had surprised the eland as it approached the streambed below the small valley. As it leapt up the bank, it was seized on the flanks by Furaha, after which, I guessed from the signs on the ground, a great struggle had taken place between them. In the struggle, Furaha had shifted her position, moving to grip its muzzle, clasping her jaws around its nasal passages and mouth, slowly suffocating the eland to death. She was alone when she came across the eland as she had separated from Batian and Rafiki to seek out one of the Zimmales. Her brother and sister did, however, find her the following day (with a little help from myself) and partook of the feast with an unprotesting, very full Furaha.

On another occasion, I radio tracked the lions to the Pitsani stream where I found them lying somewhat expectantly and quiet on the banks. I walked up to where they lay and was surprised that they did not rise to greet me, then realised their positioning formed points of a triangle around an old aardvark hole. Clearly something was within the hole's dark depths. I had no rifle as I had had to return the original rifle which was on loan. I therefore patrolled the bush armed only with a spear and, with this in hand, I decided to stamp my foot behind the entrance of the burrow. As I did this, a large male warthog literally shot out of the hole. It was as if it had been launched by a canon.

Furaha leapt forward and astonished me by seizing the warthog in mid-air, her claws latching on to its tough grey skin. Without thinking, I too jumped forward, presumably driven by my own predatory spirit, and thrust my spear into the warthog's chest as it struggled to get free of Furaha. I then stepped back as Rafiki and Batian moved forward. I watched as Furaha then changed her position and took hold of the warthog's throat to pinch its windpipe, denying it of air. It died soon afterwards. I expected the lions, with the warthog dead, to bundle forward and feed immediately and competitively. This did not happen, though. Batian and Rafiki, respecting Furaha's growling possession of the kill, moved away to watch from the shade. In time, she began to open the warthog's soft parts, but later as the sun began to beat down, she also sought the shade. At this, Rafiki rushed forward to take possession and dragged it beneath a mopane bush, ate some of it before also losing interest and moving away. I should add that the lions were already full, having killed successfully the night before.

Now all three lions lazed in the shade. I eyed the warthog; Julie and I had not had fresh meat for some time. Besides, was I not a member of this pride as well? I walked up to the warthog, took out my knife and began to slice away at the skin. Aware of my activity, Batian lifted his head and sleepily watched me. Then he pulled himself upright, stretched, yawned and began plodding towards me, without any sign of aggression. I must add that he reached me before I had secured any of the meat. I stood and watched as he then lowered his head, seized the warthog from where it lay at my feet and took it slowly back to where he had been resting. There, he pulled the warthog beneath the bushes and slumped to the ground with a contented sigh and closed his eyes.

Smiling at what I had just witnessed, I walked back to camp. When I returned later in the day, I was surprised to see that the warthog was all but consumed. Although full in the morning, a few short hours had passed and the lions had obviously felt sufficiently peckish to tackle the warthog. Julie and I ate once again from a tin that night.

It was the time of the summer rains again – the time of birth. Impala babies appear in profusion as the rain-revived grass grows long and green beside the stream banks. These babies are heavily preyed upon by a diversity of meat-eaters. The great martial eagles, Africa's largest eagle, with their hooded black heads, fall upon the new-borns. Spotted hyena nose out, then chase and quickly run down the impala young. Cheetah will catch them alive and present the babies to their cubs so that they may gain valuable experience in killing. Pythons, led by tongues which, due to the secretion of a chemical from an organ in their mouths, literally taste what is around them, also find the babies. And, of course, lions too exploit the sudden profusion of easy prey – as I witnessed one morning with Rafiki.

I heard Rafiki calling east of the camp. I looked for her, then saw her moving south. When I caught up with her, we walked on together. We had just moved into an open area when suddenly Rafiki stopped, raised her head, her ears cocked, in the direction in which she stared. I followed her gaze and saw a jackal running in fast circles after a young impala. Several times, it almost caught the baby who by now had begun emitting loud distress calls. Clearly its mother was not nearby, otherwise she or the herd male would have responded to the cries and rushed forward to chase away the jackal.

This baby was doomed, but it was not to be killed by the jackal. Rafiki began trotting and then rushed forward. As I watched, the jackal let out its own distress call when, to its absolute shock, it discovered Rafiki approaching quickly. The jackal spun and screamed away, losing in a split second its dignity as the hunter became the hunted. When I too rushed up, I saw Rafiki standing beside the impala, which was obviously exhausted and in shock. It was a strange and unsettling sight – Rafiki so powerful next to a creature so small, young and vulnerable. For some minutes, Rafiki pawed at, then chased and played with the impala (just as a domestic cat will do with a still-living mouse or small bird). After this, to my relief, she quickly killed it and began to feed.

To see Rafiki 'play' with the impala disturbed me. I realise, though, that this reaction may seem at odds with my involvement in the killing of the warthog. Pondering on how I reacted on these two occasions, I realise that the emotions I felt were fuelled by separate instincts. When with the lions, hunting adult prey, I am caught up with their need to kill. The lions live by a simple equation and I found myself, to the greater part while with them, living out that same equation. Prey must die for predators to live. I say 'to the greater part' because, as with the baby impala, there were times when I found myself emotionally unable to cope with what I saw. For example, when the lions played with baby baboons, sometimes I intervened.

I remember one such occasion distinctly. Once with the lions, we surprised a large troupe of baboons. They scattered, but two youngsters were left behind, trapped in a small tree. The lions singled the babies out and encircled the tree. The babies screamed as they jumped to miss the lions' swipes and each time they screamed, the family troop would bark in uproar and protest and advance to where I was with the lions.

One baby was seized and quickly killed by Furaha, the other was knocked to the ground by Batian. Then he began playing with it. The baby was hooked and tugged by his half-exposed claws. Its screams and cries shook me, as did its family's protesting barks at its distress. Batian stood over the baby and it peered up at him, then me, with petrified eyes, eyes that haunted me. I could not let the torment continue. The baboon was by this time also badly injured. I could suddenly stand it no longer. I stepped to one side of Batian, picked up a rock, moved forward and killed the baby.

Batian did not react aggressively, but I had broken a rule; I had interfered with his prey. He just nosed the baby before flipping it across the sand from side to side with his paws. The baby's torment was now over. Emotionally, I knew I had done all I could for it. I knew I could not have rescued the baby from Batian. Firstly, it could have been dangerous and secondly, there had been no malice in what Batian had been doing. He had simply reacted instinctively to a situation.

The human response to seeing a baby animal in pain or danger is to help or rescue it. This response had prevailed in rescuing Noko, the porcupine, for example, and of course had also prompted me to care for the lions.

However, with large prey, the lions were quick, in comparison, in killing their catch. I discovered that when my lions hunted large prey (such as eland) as a pride, the prey was immobilised by what I can only describe as a 'giant bite' on the vertebrae just behind the shoulder-blade. When inspecting these wounds, I would always think that if it was not known that lions were responsible for such an injury, one would assume that a bullet of a heavy-calibre rifle had smashed into the vertebrae. These 'giant bites' demonstrate the power and strength these great cats possess, power and strength they rarely employ.

*   *   *

By now, our Tuli Lion Trust anti-poaching team was well-established and was led by my ex-camp assistant, Mafika Manyatsa. Mafika and the team were doing excellent work, patrolling the entire range of my lions, as well as additional areas. They were the guardians of a land and wildlife much neglected in the past. Many wire snares were being pulled up, ambushes set and poachers apprehended. Mafika kept a daily diary of the team's findings, which in turn formed the basis of a section on poaching in my monthly reports for the Department of National Parks and Wildlife Management.

One morning, as I set out with a new guard to familiarise him with a valley which leads to the Shashe river – an area often used by poachers – we heard a lion calling in the distance ahead of us, and I wondered which lion it was. A few kilometres further on, we approached a thick section of bush and the new guard moved some two hundred metres to my left to check for snares. Suddenly, I heard the startled grunt of a lion. Then I saw a young male rushing out of the thick bush into which the guard had gone. The lion tore past me in long bounds, but did not see me as I stood peering from behind a huge leadwood tree. As it disappeared, I moved across to find the new guard. I found him as he was walking out towards an open area. I called to the guard and saw that he looked somewhat shocked. Certainly he would not have imagined coming across a lion on foot at close quarters on his second day of work. As I caught up with him and calmed him down, I asked what had happened. He replied that as he was checking in the dense bush for snares, he came upon a lion close by, fast asleep. The lion then awoke, saw him and fled – which is often the case when lions see man on foot in the bush and are surprised.

We continued on towards a camp at which we planned to take a short break. As we walked I asked the guard whether he had seen any sign of a collar on the lion. He said not. I had seen enough of the lion only to recognise that it had been a young male of Batian's size and age, but it had been travelling in such a blur of speed that I could not see whether or not it had a collar.

Upon reaching the camp, I decided to return alone to where the lion had fled. I wanted to make absolutely sure the lion was not Batian. At the spot, I followed the exaggerated spoor on the ground where the lion had run. As I tracked, I moved towards bush that was very dense and with caution, I decided to stop. I thought that if it was Batian who had been startled, he would respond and appear from the thick bush ahead if I called. I then began calling, 'Batian, Batian. Come on, Batian' – and waited and watched. I called again. No reply or any sign of Batian. I was beginning to feel a little foolish. Obviously the guard and I had seen a young Tuli lion. Then, as I turned to move away, I heard a soft call. I saw Batian's head protruding quizzically from some bushes. I called him, and he very nervously came out, peering everywhere but at me. He was looking for humans. He then, with a mixture of relief and affection, threw himself at me in greeting. Afterwards, he leapt effortlessly up on to a tall termite mound to scan for what he clearly feared – man. Although he had obviously been frightened on seeing the guard, I was immensely pleased with the way he had reacted – exactly as any wild lion would under similar circumstances.

Apart from the active presence of the Tuli Lion Trust's anti-poaching team, very little other anti-poaching work was taking place in the rest of the reserve. As a result of this lack of protection, snaring tragedies continued to occur. One of the saddest was the snaring of a young giraffe in late November.

Game guides from the Tuli Safari Lodge reported to me that they had consistently seen a young giraffe with a snare deeply embedded into its lower neck. It had somehow broken the wire from where it would have been attached to a tree, and the snare's 'tail' hung loose as it walked. Snares are so indiscriminate in claiming victims. The snare would have been set at a level for impala or kudu. Somehow the giraffe – an animal not deliberately targeted by that form of poaching – had, presumably when feeding on low browse, placed its head and neck unknowingly through the loop of wire. The panic and pain would then have begun.

I asked for my veterinary friend from South Africa, Andrew McKenzie, to come to the bushlands to attempt to dart and treat the giraffe. Fortunately, on the day of Andrew's arrival, the game guides had successfully managed to locate the giraffe. The darting operation went well. Andrew managed to shoot a tranquillising dart into the giraffe and it quickly succumbed to the drug. We rushed forward as it staggered on to the ground and on reaching it, we held its upper body and neck upright. We were horrified at the extent of the wound that had been inflicted by the poacher's snare. The snare had created a gross 'fold' of skin to crumple above where it was embedded in the giraffe's flesh. The snare itself was not a single-strand type, but a multi-strand cable – strong enough to tow a vehicle. How the giraffe had managed to break a trap of such strength is impossible to imagine.

Despite the seriousness of the wound, Andrew felt confident that after treatment the giraffe would have a good chance of complete recovery. He removed the snare, cleaned the wound, applied antibiotic powder, gave the giraffe an antibiotic injection and then the antidote to the tranquilliser. The young giraffe quickly rose to its feet and moved away.

From time to time, I come across this giraffe in the bush. The wound healed well, though the scarring on its neck where the poacher's snare had encircled and then eaten into its flesh will always remain. After the darting, Andrew said that, left untreated, the giraffe would probably have lived for a maximum of six weeks before succumbing fatally to blood poisoning and infection.

The snared giraffe was not the only animal Andrew and I darted together in our quest to help victims of poaching. On a table across from where I am sitting is the skull of a lioness. Seeing her skull reminds me of the saddest story about the effects of poaching on a Tuli lion. The story is of a lioness I had named Geniessa; it is her skull upon the table.

Geniessa was a member of old Darky's Lower Majale pride, and soon after I first arrived in the Tuli bushlands as a young game guide in 1983, she was caught around her neck by a poacher's snare. At the time she was also pregnant. My colleagues and I managed to release the snare which was deep within the flesh of her neck. She recovered and gave birth later to three cubs. Ten months later, all three cubs were dead. The first cub was killed outright during a conflict between her mother and a male. Another succumbed to fatal wounds received during the same incident, while the third and last, a little female, was presumed to have been deserted by Geniessa as it was never seen again.

Twenty-two months later, Geniessa stumbled into an old cable snare. The snare had long ago been pulled to the ground by feeding elephants and, like so many such snares, it had been long forgotten by the poachers who had originally set it. The snare encircled her paw and she must have fought the wire as if it were a live thing, biting not only at the snare but also at her own limb. Through gnawing, clawing, biting and tearing, she somehow released herself and blood poured from her paw. The paw was dreadfully injured. Each of the first four digits of her paw, with her claws, were torn away, leaving raw, exposed bones jutting from red flesh and tattered skin and fur.

It took many days for me to find Geniessa, but one morning, I found some distinctive dragging marks – the terrible trademark Geniessa's wound left in the sand as she walked on the remnants of her paw. I followed the tracks and, a little later, came across her beside a water-hole. Upon seeing me, she slowly moved off.

Andrew was a resident vet in the Tuli bushlands at that time and upon sighting Geniessa, I called him on my vehicle's radio and briefly explained the situation. Andrew and other staff members came quickly to where I waited. He then set out to dart Geniessa. The dart flew and hit the lioness, and on its impact and to my joy, I saw that she ran. She ran despite the injured paw. She ran, as far as I was concerned, with hope for the future. My heart was hopeful that after treatment and with care, she would survive.

Once the drug had taken effect, we examined Geniessa and suggestions regarding her future were put forward. One was that the grossly injured paw should be amputated, another was that she should be given drugs and left to recover, or not, by her own means – whichever nature wished. Our manager mentioned euthanasia and I strongly appealed against it.

The final decision concerning Geniessa was not made by Andrew or me and today this decision still sickens me. I felt at the time that no matter how grisly the wound, she should ultimately be given the chance to survive. In most situations, nature must be allowed to act unhindered by man, but I felt that if an animal had been injured through man's interference, man must again interfere to try to ensure the survival and recovery of the animal concerned.

That day, as I drove away to my camp, not knowing what the ultimate decision would be, leaving Geniessa with Andrew and the other staff, I looked at the lioness for the last time. I felt I was deserting her. Later I heard that the decision had been taken to put her down, a decision that epitomises man's conflict with nature and ultimately with himself.

Andrew carried out a post-mortem on Geniessa's body. He

discovered that apart from sustaining several broken ribs during the first snaring incident nearly two years earlier, she had at that time also broken her neck. The joint between the atlas and axis vertebrae of her backbone had snapped. But despite this, amazingly, as time passed, the joint had regrown and reformed. Andrew's discovery also ironically illustrated the terrible wounds lions can sustain, recover from and ultimately survive to live normal lives.

Today her skull stares sightlessly from the table. This lioness and her story, though, can never be forgotten. Her skull, her remains, represent, to me at least, the constant struggle to be continued against poachers, the struggle to convince others of the desperate need for compassionate custodianship which at the time of writing is so lacking in the Tuli bushlands.

One evening at the end of January 1991, Julie and I were sitting together quietly talking when all three lions suddenly appeared after being away for a few days. I went outside and walked up to them as they drank thirstily from the water drum I provided for them. As usual, they greeted me affectionately, jostling with each other for my attention. During the greeting ceremony, I suddenly noticed that a large fluid-filled membrane was hanging from Rafiki's vulva. Initially, I thought she was in the early or medium stage of pregnancy and was aborting. I was very concerned as I feared that if she was miscarrying, her life could be endangered by blood loss or infection.

Occasionally, she would turn to lick at the membrane, but otherwise she did not seem to be affected in any way and she later happily bounded off with the other two in the twilight. The following morning, I set out early to search for her, but without success. That afternoon, as I recommenced my search, I quite suddenly came across her alone, not far from the camp. She quite simply just appeared in front of me. I immediately noticed that there was no sign of the hanging membrane or any bleeding, and I sighed with relief. She was incredibly exuberant, but seemed reluctant to return with me to camp, Instead, in her own special way of calling and skipping, she made it clear that she wished me to follow her. This I did for a while, but the sun was lowering and after a time, I reluctantly had to turn back to reach camp before dark. I returned to camp alone, but a little later, Rafiki reappeared. Batian had also arrived at camp earlier. To both of us, Rafiki began to show signs that she again wished to be followed.

That night, both Batian and she slept right beside the camp's fence on the side closest to my tent. Julie and I discussed and pondered on the situation, but could not come to any conclusion as to what was going in. We both suspected that she may have miscarried, but this did not explain why she wanted Batian and I to follow her.

I awoke early the following morning and as soon as Rafiki saw me, she repeated the behaviour of the day before. She wished to be followed. This Batian and I did. We followed her for an hour or so to the west. She would return to us, calling, whenever we lagged behind, particularly so when Batian would decide to lie up and rest whenever he came across inviting shade. Rafiki led us up on to the western plateau and, followed first by Batian and then me, she entered a particularly thick section of bush along a small crevice. I then saw her climb down into a thicket and, now hidden, she began calling plaintively. Batian reacted by venturing towards where she was hidden. He peered downwards to where she lay, and stood there for a little time before moving backwards and lying down.

As he moved aside, I went forward. I peered down into the thicket and saw Rafiki nestled in her hiding place with a perfectly formed, though still, cub between her paws. I crouched just feet away and looked at the cub. Its body was completely clean and there was no sign of other cubs, blood or afterbirth. I felt a strange mixture of emotions as I crouched there. I felt great sadness for Rafiki that her cub was dead. I was deeply moved that she had wanted Batian and me to see the little one, and yet, mingled with this was my relief of the night before that Rafiki was in good health.

A little later, typical of lion mothers if their young are born dead or died soon after birth, Rafiki began to eat the little one.

After an hour, I left Batian and her and returned to camp, and there I shared what I had seen with Julie. We discussed the death of the cub. I felt it had been stillborn. Rafiki's teats had not become swollen prior to or after the birth, while in normal circumstances, lionesses' teats become noticeably heavy just prior to giving birth. Rafiki was very young to give birth. She was only thirty months old. Usually, lionesses first become pregnant at approximately forty-three months. On checking some records, however, we noted that George had documented that two of his lionesses gave birth at thirty-seven and forty-one months respectively.

Within eight days of the birth of the cub, Rafiki once again came into oestrus and mated with the larger of the two Zimmales. In total, I recorded mating taking place over three periods – at the end of January, the beginning of February and in the third week of February.

During the latter period of mating, I drove out one morning to where, some two kilometres north of camp, I heard mating snarls. There, on the border road dividing the Botswana and Zimbabwe bushlands, I came across the Zimmale and, behind him, Rafiki. I saw the Zimmale crouch to the ground as I slowly approached. I stopped as males are sometimes aggressive during a mating period. I then turned the vehicle and left them.

That afternoon, I decided (on reflection very unwisely) to return to where I had seen the lions. I took Julie with me, hopefully to photograph their courtship and mating. I felt that because it was extremely hot and if I kept a good distance from them, it would be unlikely that the Zimmale would become aggressive. I underestimated this roguish young lion and was soon to learn a lesson.

Julie and I sighted Rafiki and the Zimmale lying in scant shade where I had left them much earlier in the day. I slowed the vehicle (I was using my small open jeep) some eighty metres from them and positioned the jeep so that Julie had a clear view to take photographs if they began courting. No sooner had I stopped than I saw Zimmale's head begin to lower and then he sprang forwards and tore towards the jeep. I started the engine and turned the jeep as fast as possible so that my side was facing his charge. This was no mock display he was exhibiting. He uttered no hoarse grunts, he just continued onwards at great speed. All this happened in a flash. I realised that I had no option but to swing the little jeep towards him as I knew I had no chance of outspeeding him.

I swung the jeep hard towards him. From about two metres away, my actions caused him to swerve, then swing behind the jeep. I then shouted at him at the top of my voice and put my foot firmly down on the accelerator. He had stopped as I drove away, but I expected to see him, as I turned to look, coming after us again. Instead, I saw him staring to my right. He was looking at Rafiki, who was trotting away. Her movements had distracted him, and this action of hers allowed Julie and me to escape.

As we bounded onwards, Julie turned to me and with strange calm (what I termed 'bloody unnatural calm' at the time) said, 'Gareth, you've gone completely white.' I was indeed very shaken by what had occurred. Our eagerness to document photographically Rafiki and Zimmale together could have cost us our lives. I have no doubt that if, firstly, I had not swung the jeep in desperation at Zimmale, and secondly, he had not been distracted by Rafiki, he would have leapt into the little jeep. No small wonder I had gone white!

A few weeks later, while with Rafiki south of Tawana, I noticed that her coat had become silky – a possible indication that she was again pregnant. Also, for some time she had not sought out the Zimmales to mate with. I felt sure she was indeed pregnant. This was to prove to be correct.

That afternoon, after returning to camp, I shared my thoughts with Julie. Together, that evening, we consulted our records of when Rafiki had last mated and made calculations to estimate when she might give birth. The gestation period of lions is only one hundred and ten days.

It was several days later when, to my utter surprise, Julie told me that she felt that she too might be pregnant!

The following day, I had phone calls to make and drove down to the Pont Drift borderpost. In the cable-car shed, amongst the people I telephoned was my veterinarian friend, Andrew McKenzie. I wanted to tell him about Rafiki's early stage of pregnancy. As we spoke, I realised that he would also be the man to talk to about Julie's possible pregnancy – he after all was not only a veterinarian, but a father too. He seemed, for a moment, a little taken aback when I began talking about our suspicions, but with a chuckle, he was soon giving me details on what signs we should look for – as a father, of course, not as a veterinary practitioner.

As the days passed, Julie became almost certain that she was pregnant. This, coupled with Rafiki's condition, stirred within me an emotion all fathers-to-be must feel. Julie and I were not married. In the purest sense (and perhaps the most unrealistic sense), despite Julie's possible pregnancy, this did not now become an issue. In fact, I cannot recall either of us speaking of this. Julie then left to go to Johannesburg, having made an appointment to see a doctor some time previously concerning a minor ailment. At this appointment, she told her doctor that she thought she might be pregnant. The doctor then did a physical examination and later said that she was certainly showing all the physical signs of pregnancy.

Her breasts had become fuller and her tummy, normally so flat, certainly appeared to be somewhat distended. After she had returned to Tawana, every night Julie would proudly show me her tummy, and in the candlelight, I would look carefully and each night proclaim that indeed it looked like it was getting bigger! Were we to have a cub of our own? Julie was at this time filled with great joy – perhaps the happiest I had ever seen her at Tawana.

The subsequent use of a home pregnancy kit confused us though, as it did not really indicate clearly whether Julie was pregnant or not. We discussed our suspicions with just a handful of our Motswana friends in the Tuli who had so often in the past enquired as to why we had no children. Happy wide smiles spread across the faces of those we told.

We decided to make an appointment with a doctor in the town of Pietersburg two hundred and fifty kilometres away in the northern Transvaal so that Julie could have a scan. We were on tenterhooks as we sat in the waiting-room. Eventually, Julie was called, and together we went through to where she was to be scanned. I peered at the monitor screen that with today's incredible technology was about to reveal all. The doctor checked and examined, and Julie and I stared at the screen, trying to work out the shapes we saw. Then, rather suddenly, the doctor announced that Julie was in fact not pregnant! I asked him why she was showing the physical signs of pregnancy and he spoke of the phenomenon of phantom pregnancy. We left, quiet, minds filled with our separate thoughts.

On the drive back to the bushlands, we began discussing whether it was or was not just coincidence that she showed signs of pregnancy at the time of Rafiki becoming pregnant. Our excitement at the prospect of Rafiki having cubs had at that time largely dominated our conversations in the evenings. Perhaps this excitement and emotion had triggered a response within Julie.

Julie's signs of pregnancy quickly subsided. It was indeed a strange situation, one that made me feel that perhaps our lives with the lions were entwined to an extent which we could not entirely comprehend – thus explaining the phantom pregnancy. I may be wrong. If I am, it is at the very least a strange coincidence that Julie and Rafiki showed signs of early pregnancy at exactly the same time!

CHAPTER

10

Trials of the Tuskers

A man can't spend his life in Africa without acquiring something pretty close to a great affection for the elephants. Those great herds are, after all, the last symbol of liberty left among us.

Romain Grey, *Roots of Heaven*

Although this book is primarily about the lions and our lives with them, I feel the story would be lacking if I did not expand on what the Tuli area is best known for, its grey ghosts – its fascinating elephant population. The Tuli elephants that the lions, Julie and I used to come across almost daily epitomise their kind's situation throughout the African continent.

Elephants have many parallels with man. They, like us, are social animals that live in cohesive family groups. The females become sexually mature at about the same age as a young woman does. They hold great attachment and love for their close ones. They shed salt-water tears when traumatised or imprisoned. They, like us, understand death and mourn the loss of those who die. Elephants will return to the site of death and touch the bare bones of the deceased.

Our increasing understanding of elephants is helping man to realise that perhaps we are not much different in fact to many other forms of animal life; and it is because of subtle human conditioning

– not the actual facts – that we are raised to believe there is a wide gap between what is human and what is animal.

In the early eighties, when I first ventured into the Tuli area, periodic outbreaks of ivory poaching became a major concern. The AK47 assault rifle was in the past a symbol of liberation in Africa. Today, in post-independence times, the AK47 has become a symbol of terror. These weapons are still plentiful and in clandestine shadows change hands for low sums. The AK47 has had an enormous impact upon the African elephant and a host of other animals. In the late seventies, it was estimated that some 1.25 million elephants existed on the continent. Today their numbers are estimated at about 650,000.

Tuli elephants were also slaughtered by those with the AK47. I remember during one patrol along the Pitsani in the 1980s, I came across five dead elephants, heads carved open and their tusks extracted. Faint footprints in the dust showed the poachers' trail, but by the time I discovered the legacy of their work, these men would have been far away across in Zimbabwe or lost, in the evidence sense, in the cattle-posts to the west. One of the dead elephants I found was a pregnant female. In the dark of night, hyenas had been drawn by the gargantuan feast of flesh and had gathered, ripped and fed. I found her with her near-to-being-born calf protruding from her, mutilated by the feeding scavengers. Another sickening sight I would come across was that of elephants wounded by the poachers and only slowly succumbing to the ironical relief of death.

One morning, while guiding visitors through the reserve, I came across a large elephant bull. He walked stiffly and I approached to investigate. Suddenly, he sensed my presence, and although crippled by bullets, he attempted to charge me, but his rush was no more than a heart-wrenching slow shuffle. I notified the game department rangers, but later in the day the bull could not be found. Two days later, I found the bull. It lay dead and rotting in thick bush. The lingering death he endured was unimaginable.

Since that time, the international ban on the trade in ivory has been implemented – not a pleasing situation to many southern African conservationists. The 'If it pays, it stays' mentality is deeply ingrained, 'management' and 'utilisation' of wildlife being the general outlook. In short, 'economics'. Elephants are routinely culled in the Kruger National Park situated some two hundred and eighty kilometres east of the Tuli bushlands. 'Culled' should read 'murdered' in my opinion. Because of economic gain, plus the belief that elephant numbers in the Park should be maintained at an 'acceptable' level in relationship to available habitat, family herds are driven by helicopters above them to the killing fields. The elephants, in great terror, are then darted with a muscle-relaxant drug. Bundling together in defensive groups with calves encircled, the elephants then succumb to the drug. Certain babies are spared for a fate perhaps worse than death. These babies then witness their entire family – their mothers, brothers and sisters – being destroyed, as men on the ground step forward to deliver shots to the brains of the others, who see and experience all but are unable to flee because of the paralytic effect of the drug. These practices, in my opinion, represent modern man as the savage and the age-old elephant as the civilised.

The baby elephants are then transported away to later be sold. These babies were, up until very recently, sold to zoos and circuses – a lifetime of imprisonment. Today, the practice is to sell them off to other reserves for 'restocking'. It seems that such restocking, using orphans of the Kruger killing fields, is a further stress-inflicting exercise. On release, they often become very elusive – fleeing on hearing a vehicle and remaining in the most inaccessible (for man) parts of these reserves. It is much like taking highly traumatised human children and putting them into an environment without adult protection, care and guidance. The mental scars will run deep. Incidentally, in the Kruger, it has been discovered that due to the annual offtake of elephants, the females are producing young at an earlier age, as if the population is attempting to balance the damage of the killing fields.

The renowned elephant expert and elephant 'mother', Daphne Sheldrick – who in Kenya was the first person to successfully rear newborn elephant and rhino orphans – has taught me through her written and spoken words of the true needs of these beings, which she describes as 'human animals', and their deservedness of quality of life. Daphne and her colleagues in Kenya have illustrated how in large reserves, elephants are not the 'animal bulldozers' described by some, or the 'destroyers of habitat' often referred to, but, in fact, are the 'gardeners of Eden'.

In the vast Tsavo National Park, over a forty-year period, Daphne and her colleagues have seen how elephants recycle and reconstruct the wilds. Once in perhaps a hundred years or more, the combination of drought and the elephants' needs creates a situation of natural regulation of elephant numbers – death; which Daphne describes as humane for it is as if nature is undertaking euthanasia of the herds. Being water-dependent, the elephants in the drought stay by the rivers and cannot range in search of their full-balanced diet. Daphne told me how these elephants weaken and begin to rest and sleep more and more until death quietly passes over them. Nature's euthanasia may occur only once in one hundred years, and habitat change takes place. Because of the elephants, feeding scrub is opened up. In turn, grasslands develop. The surviving elephants once again contribute to the establishment of new trees, as seed passes through the elephants in their dung and germination occurs. Additionally, dung beetles roll the dung and bury it under the ground with their larvae, placing hundreds of tons of dung into the ground, feeding it. Nature is never static, but today some conservationists in southern Africa insist on attempting to play god, by manipulating nature to maintain the *status quo*.

Returning to the Tuli elephants, the question of 'to cull or not to cull' has often been discussed by the landowners. Fortunately, the international ivory ban has removed the financial motivation for culling the Tuli elephants and an ecological justification just does not exist if one believes in Daphne Sheldrick's philosophy. As I have mentioned, she opened my eyes and re-educated me in the true needs of elephants. This was part of a general re-education. As a result of working in wildlife predominantly within southern Africa, I found myself being tainted with subtle conditioning – a conditioning which begins to make one believe that manipulation of the wilds is viable and essential. If you hear it often enough and never hear the other side, you begin to believe it.

Today, the Tuli elephants range over a far bigger area than the combined Botswana/Zimbabwe 1,200-square-kilometre Tuli bushlands reserves, and are now recolonising areas of their former range where once their ancestors died and persecuted survivors fled from the west, north and east into the Tuli. Aerial surveys undertaken over the past ten years have shown that the actual number of elephants in the Botswana Tuli bushlands has not risen in real terms during that time, but remains fairly constant at about six hundred and fifty.

Another indication of the symbiosis of Tuli elephants and the habitat was discovered by a friend of mine, Chris Styles. Chris visited Tawana when working towards his Master's in the bushlands and was studying aspects of vegetation impact by large animals. Some people's natural reaction when seeing a tree damaged, or ring-barked or dying, is negative – thoughts like 'elephant damage', 'too many elephants', 'culling needed' spring instantly to their minds. Chris looked beyond these thoughts and discovered much. For example, there are large areas in the Tuli where stunted mopane trees occur. This stunting was attributed to 'detrimental elephant impact'. Chris discovered that eland were also responsible for the mopanes' stunted appearance. The trees are browsed upon and so never grow tall and have a hedged appearance. Instead of being negative, it is in a far-reaching way very positive. Chris discovered that late in the winter, just prior to the summer rains, when the area seems at its most desperate, these 'stunted' mopane trees suddenly burst out in leaf – much earlier than the tall mopane – with a rich and accessible food source for the host of winter-worn leaf-eaters.

The future of the Tuli elephants is as uncertain as it is in the rest of Africa. The reality of culling could one day arise, and ivory poaching could again flare up at any time. As there is at present no full-time anti-poaching work being undertaken across all of the Tuli landowners' private reserves (only in the Charter Reserve is a sizeable area being covered routinely by the team we established), the Tuli elephants are a vulnerable population. However, fortunately there is today the presence of the Botswana Defence Force unit stationed also in the Charter Reserve portion. If large-scale ivory poaching flared, this unit could be strengthened by the use of spotter aircraft.

Lastly, on the subject of the Tuli elephants and poaching, just a few months ago, a horrific by-product of poaching occurred and the following is what was recounted to me.

At a tourist camp, a strong smell of decay swirled in the air. The source of the smell was investigated and some distance from the camp was found an extremely large bull elephant, perhaps the area's largest. The bull was in extreme pain and suffering. With a mopane branch in its trunk, the bull would repeatedly scrape at its great head. Its head was fluid-filled, gangrenous and in parts writhed with maggots. The bull was destroyed and, on inspection, it was discovered that the bull's hideous state was caused by bullets – bullets that failed to penetrate the brain.

I fear for the Tuli elephants. If ivory poaching was to strike in an organised way, because of the area's general vulnerability many could die before the situation was eventually stabilised.

CHAPTER

11

A Time of Tears

... Nature, whose sweet rains fall on unjust and just
alike, will have clefts in the rocks where I may hide, and
secret valleys in whose silence I may weep undisturbed.
She will hang the night with stars so that I may walk
abroad in the darkness without stumbling, and send
the wind over my footprints so that none may track
me to my hurt.

Oscar Wilde

By May 1991, Julie and I had every reason to be pleased with the
results of our efforts for the Tuli bushlands and for the lions. The
anti-poaching team, financed and trained by us, had, in the first
five months of that year, already pulled up and removed over
five hundred poachers' snares and traps. Additionally, the team
had arrested a score of poachers who were handed over to the
police. In turn, the Tuli lion population had risen to new heights.
Eighteen months previously, only twenty-five lions existed in the
Tuli, but by May I estimated that the population, including cubs,
had risen to forty-three.

By this time, Rafiki and Furaha were fully rehabilitated, pregnant
and happy. Batian, now a beautiful, golden young prince, was
regularly disappearing north into the Zimbabwean portion of the
Tuli bushlands. He had finally found a lioness of his own. He would
return to our camp after an absence of several days, noticeably tired

but content. After these amorous sojourns in the north, Batian would greet me exuberantly, rubbing his great tawny head against me and groaning in pleasure over and over. I would see his courting scars and smile.

An initial part of lion courtship is the rebuttal behaviour exhibited by the lioness, which is later combined with hugely flirtatious advances towards the male. Batian, young and perhaps over-eager to mate during the early part of the courtship, received more swats than could be considered normal from the lioness. Nevertheless, neither this nor the resulting courting scars seemed to worry him.

So overall, as a result of all this and more, Julie and I were living in a happy time in the Tuli bushlands. Our golden time, however, was to be brief and passed all too quickly. A shadow of darkness, culminating in great sorrow and death, was about to engulf us.

The dark time began suddenly one morning late in May. At sunrise, as the sky was turning orange, I heard loud sounds of lions in conflict coming from the east. Initially, I thought it was Rafiki, Furaha and Batian having a short, sharp squabble over a kill. However, the sounds continued, deepening and intensifying; I was hearing great violence, desperation and danger. I grabbed my rifle and ran from the camp heading towards the dreadful sounds. I barely heard Julie calling to me to be careful. She had spoken aloud, but her words were a fleeting whisper in my mind. What rang loudly within me was my fear for the lions.

Two hundred yards or so from camp, just as I reached a stream bank, two golden forms dashed towards me – two lionesses. It was Rafiki and Furaha and both of them had full bellies and bloodied faces, indicating that they had recently fed. I remember letting out a sigh of relief as they greeted me with great excitement. 'They're fine,' I thought to myself.

My thoughts, as the lionesses pressed themselves against me, turned to Batian. As if reading my mind, both Rafiki and Furaha ceased their greetings and began to walk back in the direction from which they had come. What I did not realise at the time was that Batian's sisters were leading me to where he lay.

I followed the lionesses and minutes later, between the stunted mopane trees ahead, I saw three jackals. Strangely, both lionesses then circled around the area where I felt sure their kill lay. The lionesses were leading me on to higher ground when, to the south, I heard the gruff, intermittent but distant calls of two lions. On hearing the sounds, Rafiki and Furaha stopped, listened, then quickly moved away to the north. I did not follow them. I felt certain that a fight had occurred between my lions and others trespassing in their core area. I had a sinking feeling that Batian was in trouble and backtracked to the area around which the lionesses had cautiously circled and where I had seen the jackals.

I entered the area and again saw the jackals. As I approached, they spun and dashed away. It was then that I saw a lion. It lay on the ground thirty metres away, its head partially raised, but its eyes unseeing. I stopped and stared, praying that this was not what I greatly feared it must be. But it was Batian. His features and mind had been altered by shock and by gruesome physical injury. I walked up to this shadow of a lion, my lion, my Batian. I knelt in front of him, gently calling his name, touching his head, seeking to penetrate his uncomprehending mind – and then I cried. Through the tears I saw the hideous extent of his injuries. His tail had been bitten off, and lay in two broken pieces on the stony ground nearby. Only eight inches of his tail remained, bloody and pitted with deep bite marks.

I gently brushed aside Batian's mane hair and saw the wounds on the nape of his neck where long canines had been deeply buried and, when withdrawn, had left a mess of exposed, torn muscle. His tawny body was criss-crossed with long, bloody cuts, raking wounds caused by his attackers' claws.

I soon discovered what had occurred. From what I could see, it appeared that my lions were feeding upon their kill when they were surprised by the appearance of two young males. The lionesses fled as a short, savage fight took place – Batian alone against the two. He had instinctively, as is the way of a single male who is outnumbered, backed into nearby bushes to protect his back from the fatal bite to the base of the spine which his attackers would have sought to inflict. In the short battle, Batian fought with incredible courage, and the fact that he was still alive bore testament to this. But against two lions his own size, he was inevitably dealt those devastating injuries.

Batian's attackers, possibly as a result of my appearance, or more probably their territorial insecurity, quickly fled south from where they had come. It was their short calls which I had heard down the valley earlier. Contrary to what I expected, these males never returned to my lions' core area, thus proving that the incident was not territorially instigated, but a freak encounter demonstrating the cruelty of nature.

I stayed with Batian for many minutes trying to comfort him, trying too to gather my own thoughts and feelings. I knew what had to be done that could help him. I then rose and headed towards camp, my pace quickening until I found myself running as fast as I could. On reaching camp, I saw Julie in the kitchen area and stammered out what had happened. Tears again flooded my eyes. I remember saying to her in desperation, 'I think Batian's going to die.'

By a strange stroke of good fortune at a terrible time, my veterinarian friend, Andrew McKenzie, was visiting the reserve, staying at a camp which was in radio contact with us. As Julie called Andrew for help, I put a bowl and container of water into a bag and quickly returned to where Batian lay. Andrew responded to the urgency of the situation, saying he would soon be with us and would on his way pick up antibiotics from another camp.

Once with Batian again, I encouraged him to drink, but to no avail. His eyes now appeared less glazed, and I felt that through the haze of shock he was experiencing, he realised that I was with him.

Later, I heard the drone of a vehicle near camp and returned to meet Andrew. I quickly recounted to him the extent of Batian's injuries. His face was grim. I led the way on foot and Julie and Andrew followed in our Isuzu pick-up as we headed towards where Batian lay. Andrew studied Batian's condition through binoculars. He prepared a syringe with antibiotics and told Julie and me that in Batian's present state, it would be dangerous to tranquillise and move him to the safety of the enclosure at camp. The combination of shock and the drugs would be fatal.

Andrew then handed me the syringe and I walked over to Batian. Calling softly to him, I administered a large dose of antibiotics and he seemed not to notice as I pressed the needle into him. Additionally, I sprayed antibiotic powder into the wounds on his neck and the stump of his tail. I then set about trying to provide shade for him by tying an old tent, outspread, to some nearby bushes so that it hung above him providing protection from the dehydrating rays of the sun. With this achieved, I encouraged Batian to drink. Dehydration was a great fear. He barely lapped the water as I coaxed him to drink, placing the water-bowl beneath his mouth. To cool him, I trickled water on to the hair of his head and body, gently patting the fur to spread the water through his fur and on to his skin.

During the afternoon, despite his injuries, Batian showed his unbroken spirit as he rose to his feet, quivered upon his once sound legs, and tottered a few paces to the nearest clump of mopane bushes. As he reached the bushes, he crumpled to the ground and lay panting, obviously in great pain.

Andrew told Julie and me that he would return in a few days to tranquillise Batian, move him to our camp and operate upon the remnants of his tail. Firstly, though, Batian had to get over the traumatic shock he was experiencing.

That evening, I stayed with Batian to keep watch over him. I feared that hyena might be attracted to the scene of the fight or that the two young males might return. At nightfall, I placed a gas light some yards away from where I sat beside Batian. Frequently that night, I encouraged my battered friend to drink water from the white plastic bowl. No lions ventured near, nor did cackling clans of hyena, but an elephant herd caused me some anxiety late that night. I heard them quite suddenly, as is often the case with these surprisingly silent animals. I heard mopane leaves being stripped from branches by invisible trunks around us, the elephants' rumbling communication sounds reverberating through the air. The elephants had approached soundlessly, stopping to feed a small distance from where I sat. Silently I pleaded with the elephant herd to move away. Batian and I would be helpless if, catching our scent, the elephants became aggressive. Fortunately for us the herd did move off shortly and I thanked the unseen gods and began dozing intermittently.

Dawn came and I left Batian and headed for the camp. Julie had spent the night alone, but had been unconcerned about this, her thoughts being with Batian and me in the bush. Later, Julie set off to the Pont Drift borderpost and on to the small town of Alldays, a six-hour round trip, to buy meat for Batian as well as additional supplies for us. I spent the day near Batian, who had become increasingly still, although he did manage to lap water occasionally.

Late in the afternoon, after spending some time with Julie after her trip, I tried to encourage Batian to eat some meat, but he showed no interest. I noticed large metallic green-bodied flies squatting on the surrounding bushes and I winced at the sight of them. These flies lay eggs in and around any open wounds and on rotting flesh. The eggs quickly hatch into hungry, tiny maggots that feast upon flesh and in turn bloat to a size of over half an inch. I checked Batian and noticed clusters of yellow eggs near the ugly circular puncture wounds on his neck and elsewhere. Disgusted by the thought of what could occur, I began scraping the eggs away. I removed many, but some were entangled deep within Batian's mane hair.

Night fell and I sat talking to Batian to comfort him, talking about the many chapters of his life that I had shared with him. I murmured softly in the darkness to him of his struggle to succeed in becoming the prince which he was; of our times together north on the wide plateau, proclaiming in unison at dusk, for all to hear, our claim to the Tawana and Pitsani valleys; and I spoke to him of our territorial patrols together over the land we held as our pride's domain. At about two o'clock, having woken from a short sleep, I turned on my torch and checked Batian. I shone the light on his body and saw to my horror a mass of small, white maggots wriggling through his wounds. It was an appalling sight. I had some brandy in my bag and, in desperation, I poured small quantities of it into each wound. With my knife, I began scraping the maggots out and was partially successful in clearing away many of them. However, others remained deep within the puncture wounds.

The following morning, Julie set off once again on the six-hour journey in search of medicine to deal with the maggot infestation. Rafiki, looking very pregnant, had visited the camp the night before and was still nearby in the morning. While Julie was away, I led Rafiki to where her brother lay in the hope that, on seeing his sister, Batian's spirits might be bolstered. Rafiki became very nervous as we approached him. His appearance had obviously changed and he could not display his normal body language. Because of this, Rafiki was confused and growled occasionally. After a while, she lay down, staring at me beside Batian.

Julie's trip had been successful and she had managed to acquire an excellent powder to get rid of the maggots. I sprinkled this grey powder around Batian's wounds and instantly the maggots began dropping out, wriggling in Batian's fur before falling to the ground. Prior to my applying this powder, Batian had managed to stand and had attempted to stretch his aching body. He had then lain down and begun to lick his wounds – all signs that the shock was passing.

That night, I continued to encourage him to drink and, using a syringe, also trickled a mixture of rehydration solution and water into his mouth. At dawn, he lapped some more water and ate some liver, heart and kidney. Throughout the day, I trickled the rehydration liquid into his mouth. Mostly, Batian would swallow the liquid, but at times, when his spirit ebbed, he would allow the liquid to dribble out of his great mouth and to the ground, creating a wet circle upon which his chin lay.

Andrew was due to return the following day, and Batian and I spent our last night together in the bush. In the darkness beside Batian, I willed the hours to pass, but dawn, it seemed, came reluctantly. My concern for Batian was making me impatient.

My impatience was, in part, a result of tiredness and anxiety, but mostly because of a fear of losing him. He was like a first-born son to me.

According to Andrew's instructions, when the dawn did finally arrive, I did not attempt to get Batian to feed prior to his being tranquillised. Andrew arrived at our camp with Phil Khan, a wildlife photographer, who was assisting him. After a brief welcome, we headed out in our truck to Batian. I was again given the syringe, this time containing a tranquilliser, and I injected my lion. Without any sign of stress, Batian fell into a deep, unconscious state. As I signalled to the others that he was asleep, Andrew drove towards us. We rolled Batian on to a spread blanket and with each of us holding a corner, lifted him with some effort on to the back of the truck and returned to camp.

There, with Andrew muttering that the condition of Batian's tail was terrible, the first of a series of drips was set up. Andrew operated on Batian in the back of the Isuzu for two and a half hours. Much of what remained of Batian's tail had to be removed. It was gangrenous. Andrew obviously did not want to fill me with false hope. I knew that Batian's condition was precarious and Andrew told me so quite plainly, adding, however, that he was doing everything possible. Three litres of glucose drip trickled into my dehydrated lion and I willed every drop to make him stronger. After removing two vertebrae from Batian's tail, Andrew neatly stitched up the stump and set about dealing with the other injuries.

Andrew worked hard and meticulously. His increasing frown troubled me greatly. I feared what it might represent. He was visibly drained when the work was finally completed. We carried Batian to the same enclosure where, as large cubs, he and his sisters had frolicked at night a year and a half before. We left him to sleep off the effects of the drugs. After the operation, I felt more optimistic. I had enormous faith in Batian's courageous spirit and will to live.

The following morning presented Andrew with a sight which I feel he will never forget. I walked into the enclosure early, calling to Batian. To our amazement, this brave, battle-torn lion with no tail rose, and despite tottering legs, walked with determination and spirit towards where I stood – and greeted me. I looked up and out of the enclosure to where I saw Andrew and Julie standing, watching the scene. Andrew's face was radiant with smiles, as was Julie's – just as mine must have been.

I embraced him before he, with hunched back and painful body, staggered to where he knew the water-bowl was and drank and drank. Later Batian ate some meat – the first real meal he had had since the whole crisis had begun. The next day, he ate again, and even during the night, he found some meat for himself which I had left for him in the enclosure. I had previously been handing the meat to Batian, so this was the first time that he had actively sought meat to eat.

However, on the third day after the operation, his condition deteriorated. That strong spark of life within him dimmed. He drank little and did not eat. Even Rafiki's appearance at the gate of the enclosure that evening did little to lift his spirits. In desperation, and in order to get some sustenance into Batian, I mixed up six eggs in a bowl and dripped the liquid into his mouth; I remembered how, as a cub, for some reason he had relished eggs. To my astonishment and relief, he began eagerly lapping from the bowl, quickly finishing its contents. I gave him every egg we had and the following day, Julie yet again undertook the six-hour round trip to buy a large supply of eggs.

That night, Rafiki appeared at camp and drank water. She greeted me very quickly before hastily moving away, her way of indicating to me that she did not wish to be followed. Some time during the darkness of that cool night, she gave birth to four cubs. I did not see Rafiki for four more days. She remained hidden with the little ones in her well-chosen nursery site less than two kilometres away from Tawana Camp.

Over these few days, Batian's condition improved considerably. At night, he would eat almost all the meat which I left beside the blanket I had put down for him to lie on after the operation. Batian's recovery continued well as we entered a time of birth and hope.

Rafiki had not visited camp at all for five days when, one morning, I heard a lion drinking from one of the water-bowls. At first, I thought it was Batian. He was no longer restricted by injury to the enclosure, but was wandering short distances away from the camp. The sounds of lapping beckoned me and I saw Rafiki slim, but with her teats heavy with milk. She had given birth!

I immediately went out to her. To my initial surprise, she greeted me very briefly before hastily heading north. A little later, she stopped, turned, looked at me and then returned to greet me in her normal heartfelt way. After the greeting, she did not object as I followed behind her to where the little ones lay hidden. As we headed north, she would stop at intervals and turn around, allowing me to catch up. I lost her, though, in some thick bush as we reached a bend in the Tawana streambed. She had vanished, melting into the green and tawny riverine thickets. I peered around, softly calling her name. Then, to my right, I heard a faint reply in return. There, deep in a natural hollow beneath the protective branches of a buffalo thorn bush on a bank of the stream, was Rafiki. I moved forward a little, sat down, then looked in fascination. I saw her with a single, tiny cub.

I did not remain at the nursery site for long, however, as, brimming with excitement and pride, I returned to tell Julie of what I had seen. At camp, in this long-anticipated moment of shared joy, we both shed tears. Later, I returned to Rafiki, and while sitting quietly watching, I saw two more cubs, their eyes tightly closed. Sitting with them, Rafiki was the picture of completeness.

The following is an extract from my daily diary marking the special day and reflects the happiness I felt:

> It is an incredible privilege to sit upon a river bank watching a lioness with tiny cubs, without fear, just pride. It is an incredible feeling too when Rafiki leaves her cubs to greet me. It's a magical merging of our lives.

The next day, when visiting Rafiki, I saw that there were in fact a total of four cubs. One, however, was dead. I watched as Rafiki constantly licked at its mottled back and little white belly. It seemed to me that she was, through these actions, willing her cub to live.

I remembered how, five months earlier when she had given birth to a single, stillborn cub, she had naturally eaten it. She had first, though, led Batian and me into that nursery site in which the cub was born lifeless. Remembering this occasion, I expected Rafiki to eat the little one that day, but she did not. As I left her in the evening, she still licked at its body. I left thinking that if she did not eat the cub soon, its scent, as its body decomposed, could attract other predators, particularly leopard, to the nursery site. If a leopard found the cubs unattended, it would move forward to kill and eat all the cubs. Early the next morning, I headed anxiously up to the nursery site. As I approached the bend in the streambed, I heard a sound above and to the right of me. As I turned, a small leopard leapt down a nearby Scotia tree. It hit the ground and tore away at great speed across the streambed. In a flash it had disappeared.

I feared the worst. The leopard's close proximity to the nursery site spelt disaster to me. I hurriedly walked on, expecting to find a nursery site empty of cubs. To my great delight, however, I found Rafiki with the cubs clambering clumsily around her. The dead one, I noticed as I sat down, lay between her paws. Rafiki later stood, stretched her stiff body and came to greet me before she returned to the nursery site and began to lick again at the dead cub.

An hour later, she began eating the cub. Although sad, it was a remarkably natural sight. The cub was a part of Rafiki, it had been borne by her and, as I watched, she completed a short cycle, returning a part of her to herself. By so doing, the cub's nutrients, those she had provided, were returned to her. Additionally, by eating the cub, she was preventing its smell from attracting predators.

Despite Rafiki removing all traces of the dead cub, I did still fear the return of the leopard that I had seen. Had its presence merely been coincidental or had the leopard been attracted to the vicinity of the nursery by the scent of the dead cub? Would it return and patiently watch and wait out of sight for Rafiki to move away to hunt before it ventured towards the defenceless cubs? Happily, the leopard did not return and the cubs grew quickly as time passed.

During this time, Batian continually became stronger. The wounds on the nape of his neck, however, were filled with fluid and took time to drain. Each day, I would clean these injuries, but what really helped to heal these wounds was Batian himself. He would lie for hours on his back, white belly exposed and hind legs dangling comically at either side. I feel he knew that this posture was beneficial to the healing of the neck wounds as it allowed the otherwise trapped fluid to drain. Despite the fact that Batian was feeding well, I still gave him the mixture of nine or so eggs daily which he always lapped from the bowl I held beneath his white chin.

One evening, after giving Batian his eggs, Furaha appeared at camp, still very pregnant. She greeted me enthusiastically, but not so Batian. In his stiff, hunched way, he happily came forward to greet his favourite sister. At his advance, she sunk low to the ground, hissing and baring her formidable teeth. Again, it was his altered appearance and being unable to exhibit his normal behaviour which prompted Furaha's reaction. Batian persisted, though, and after initially stopping, he came forward again. Furaha's hissing intensified. I stepped backwards and she too retreated, pressing herself against me. It was a tense time. I wanted to try to pacify Furaha so that she did not strike out at her already battered brother, but just at this volatile moment, I heard the sound of a vehicle approaching camp. I groaned inwardly.

Because of the sensitivity of our work with the lions, people rarely came unannounced to the camp, and this we appreciated. It was particularly strange that a vehicle was coming at this time to our camp without any prior warning as it was known in the Tuli that things were doubly sensitive around our camp, with Rafiki with cubs, Furaha very pregnant and Batian recovering from his terrible ordeal. In short, this was a most inappropriate time for anyone, except in an emergency, to drive to the rehabilitation camp.

With Furaha still hissing beside me, I asked Julie, who was nearby watching from inside the camp, to explain the present situation to whoever was driving up to the gate, and to request that they leave. I also told her that I would meet the occupants of the vehicle at the nearby Pitsani river as soon as the lions made it possible.

Julie went to the gate, met the vehicle and passed on the message. I expected to hear the vehicle moving off, but instead heard voices becoming louder. Already feeling anxious at Batian and Furaha's interaction, I began to get angry. Julie then reappeared looking as annoyed as I felt.

'It's Mr U— [a member of the Tuli landowners' committee] and his friends. I've told him the situation and he said, "Look, tell Gareth that it's Mr U— here and we wish to come in to see Batian."'

I became livid. It had been accepted for months that the rehabilitation of the lions involved minimising contact between them and people other than ourselves. The hissing below me intensified as Batian stepped forward and I quickly asked Julie to tell Mr U— that it was impossible for him and his friends to enter the camp due to the circumstances and to repeat that I would meet them as soon as possible at the Pitsani river. Julie did this, the vehicle rumbled off and she returned looking grim.

My words, repeated by Julie, had caused the Johannesburger to lose face in front of his friends and he was angered. This incident was to add one more branch to fuel the fires of resentment shown to Julie and me by some of the Tuli landowners. It was a doubly tense time as due to an agreement (arising from the landowners committee's reaction to some of my heartfelt public opinions on situations in the bushlands), any work I wished to publish or write about the reserve, including in public interviews and in communication with the Botswana Government, now had to first be cleared by the landowners committee.

Remarkably, only three weeks after the fight and his operation, Batian was once again beginning to spend days away from the vicinity of Tawana Camp. His dreadful wounds were healing well, he gained much weight and once again, his muscles became well defined and taut. It was thought by some that he would never again lead the life of a wild lion and I was told that the loss of his tail would severely affect his balance.

However, Batian adapted, and in time could run strongly, apparently unaffected in any way. One effect of the loss of his tail was that he could no longer flick the irritating flies from his back. As flies settled, his sorry stump of a tail would waggle and the flies would remain, plaguing him with their persistent pin-prick stings. When seeing this, I would, with wry sadness, brush the flies away.

Batian's body healed well and I was constantly amazed by his courageous spirit which, despite his near death ordeal, had remained unbroken. He did not, as a result of the fight and trauma, become a nervous, dispirited male, territorially insecure, and constantly watchful and fearful of trespassing males. Instead, as the wounds healed, he began to call loudly, advertising his presence to all who could hear him for kilometres around, and once again, he began scent-marking and jetting on his favourite bushes. Batian was restating his ownership of the Tawana and Pitsani valleys.

I was proud and relieved to see this behaviour. Batian was teaching me, through his fight, his recovery and bold territorial action, true courage, a courage which, in the weeks and months ahead, I drew from to enable me in turn to cope with a great calamity and grief.

Returning to his sisters, one evening when Batian was in the north, no doubt again seeking 'his' lioness, I led Furaha up to Rafiki and the cubs in the nursery site. As Rafiki accepted me so completely, I presumed she would act in a similar way to the rest of her pride. As we approached the nursery, I noticed Furaha beginning to deliberately lag behind me, looking around anxiously. At first I thought that she had perhaps scented the leopard and I walked on expecting her to catch up. Then I saw Rafiki looking at me from within the nursery. I called softly and went to sit down. As I did so, I turned and saw Furaha behind me, still nervous. Abruptly, as I sat, she sat. I understood that it was because she was at the nursery site that she was nervous. Later, I rose and Furaha rose and, close together, we walked up on to the stream bank to my 'cub-viewing' point. When I reached the spot, I sat down and, to my surprise, Furaha lay herself partially over my legs. Rafiki watched her sister closely, once or twice raising her upper lip in a grimace to momentarily reveal a canine – lion language indicating mild annoyance. I was learning that according to lion etiquette, or certainly Rafiki's, it was not appropriate for a sister to visit another when cubs are still very small. Furaha and I rose and moved away.

Furaha walked with her body against my legs and did not give her sister a backward glance. She was relieved we were leaving. Only once we were well away from the nursery did Furaha's behaviour change and once again, she became jaunty and confident, two of her typical characteristics.

Fortunately, both lionesses' attitude towards their brother altered as he got better. All hissing and snarling became a thing of the past and their robust, playful nature towards him again prevailed. One evening, I watched with joy as Batian greeted Furaha. She rubbed her head against his, then playfully slapped at him before leaping momentarily on to his great shaggy head. She skipped away, but deliberately not fast enough so that he could catch up with her. Then they tumbled, sniffed and played, behaviour reminiscent of their adolescence when they were large cubs. Another evening, I watched Batian eyeing Rafiki as she crouched to drink and began lapping water from the drum. He moved purposefully towards her and, much to my amusement, he then attempted to mate with her. Rafiki alternated between lapping thirstily (she hadn't drunk for two days) and twisting around, hissing, with drenched chin, to deter Batian from his attempts to mate.

Furaha gave birth a month after Rafiki. Typical of her independent nature, she did not give birth nearby, but some eight kilometres away to the east of camp. One day, she, like Rafiki, appeared at camp no longer pregnant, but thirsty and heavy with milk, approximately five days after the birth of the cubs. After I had spent two days searching for her nursery site, she eventually led me to the cubs. I followed her tracks up on to the eastern escarpment, across the topmost section of Poachers' Valley, then up again on to a rocky plateau that overlooked the wide Shashe valley. There, because of the hard orange stones covering the ground, I lost her tracks. I peered into gulleys and crevices for an hour without success. Then, quite suddenly, I heard her calling me and saw her about a hundred and fifty metres away in an opening. After we greeted, she led me into another stony gulley and, as Rafiki had done, stopped to allow me to catch up with her. Once in the gulley, I walked close behind her. She veered to the right, stepped over some branches and there were her cubs. Shafts of yellow light bounced off their little mottled forms and three squirming little cubs noisily made it clear that they were glad their mother had come back.

Furaha's nursery site was quite different in many ways to Rafiki's. This too highlighted the fundamental differences between the two sisters. Furaha's nursery was not completely shaded and, unlike Rafiki's, no soft soil lay beneath the cubs, only slabs of stone and old branches. One factor in common with both nursery sites, however, was the fact that they were well concealed.

142

Furaha too accepted my presence completely. She settled upon the uncomfortable stones and, with me watching from a distance of three paces, began cleaning the cubs who, despite being less than a week old, made loud protestations. After their bath, they crawled to her teats and suckled and then slept – three little bundles of brown and gold nestled securely close beside their mother.

By July, Batian had completely recovered from his wounds and, to my surprise, began frequently heading south down the Pitsani valley into the Lower Majale pride's territory which old Darky had reigned over for the past ten years. Darky had had an unusually long tenure as pride male. He was indeed a special lion, but Batian's persistence in venturing south indicated that the old king's reign was ending and my young prince was seeking to take his place at the head of the pride's hierarchy.

In life, Darky was shrouded in mystery. Somehow, for so long, he had escaped the South African hunters' guns and the poachers' numerous snares. He seemed at times an immortal being, living on while man killed many of his lionesses, daughters and sons. The old man constantly escaped the dangers, somehow surviving over the long years.

Darky's disappearance too was mysterious. No remains of his body were ever found – he simply vanished and was never seen again. With this, Batian roamed without fear in the old pride master's land. It is possible that the South African hunters from across the river finally claimed Darky, using baits and feeding sounds as they have for years to lure lions to their deaths. I prefer to think, though, that old Darky simply passed away. He was, by 1991, about sixteen years old, a great age for a male lion in the wilds. Most male lions die or disappear at the age of eight years, the natural pressures or man's activities determining their fates. Perhaps Darky simply died in a quiet part of his territory in the Tuli bushlands. He left a legacy, though – his blood flows in the majority of the Tuli lions, most of the population being directly or indirectly related to the old man. Even Rafiki's and Furaha's cubs were related to Darky – their father, 'Zimmale', was in all probability one of Darky's sons.

On his visits to Tawana, Batian would be subjected to much curious sniffing from his sisters. Furaha and Rafiki would keenly nose him, learning from the scent upon him who he had been

143

mating and associating with. Part of me was pleased for Batian, seeking to take the place of Darky, but I also held grave fears for him. The southern part of the Lower Majale pride's territory bordered with the usually dry Limpopo river, across which a land of man, game ranches and guns existed. Because of my fears, I would track and search for Batian when he ventured near the Limpopo. On these occasions, I would normally find him lying sprawled beneath a Shepherds tree on the plains. I would walk up to my friend, receive an enthusiastic greeting, then sit beside him in the circle of shade until the sun lowered and the air cooled. Then I would rise, stroke his great head, and walk northwards towards Tawana. Batian would follow, he and I heading north on the wide plains, our backs to the dangerous world of man to the south.

On other occasions, I would find Batian's tracks in the south and, from my vehicle and the top of low hills, I would call him as I proceeded northwards. Late at night, responding to my calls, he would appear at camp, and as I awoke in turn to his calls, I would go to him, stroke his head and silently wish he would remain and not return to the dangers of the south. But, of course, it was natural for him to seek females. He was instinctively reacting to the demise of a pride male. Nature abhors a vacuum and Batian, by moving south, was preventing a non-productive vacuum from forming.

Late in July, a sub-group of the Lower Majale pride suddenly crossed the Limpopo into South Africa. I have no doubt that they were lured by baits and feeding sounds played through powerful speakers by the hunters. It was reported to me that one young lioness had been run over and killed by a vehicle and another had been illegally shot. I reacted to these reports by contacting the relevant government authorities and individuals in Botswana and South Africa. I urgently proposed that the remaining members of the Lower Majale sub-group be darted and relocated back to the Tuli bushlands. One morning, I learnt that some of the lions had been sighted on a game farm situated ten kilometres south of the Limpopo. I phoned the manager of this farm and asked him to give me time to organise the relocation. He agreed.

The evening of that same day, he and the owner of the game farm shot and killed a young male lion which they had lured and baited with a donkey carcass.

They shot Batian dead.

'The lion had no tail.' These words haunt me and will continue to haunt me for ever. It was confirmed to me later that 'the lion had no tail'.

I cannot describe our grief. It was, and still is, too deep.

On the day that I learnt it was Batian who had been murdered, I walked out of our camp and headed down to the confluence of two streams. Upon the bank where the streams meet there is a tall Scotia tree alongside a rain tree and beneath these is a small water-hole. It is a place where, in the past, the lions and I would frequently rest, facing the west and the lowering sun.

It is a place of many memories, a peaceful place. That day, I dug a grave near the two trees and collected piles of pretty stones from the streambeds. I did not have my lion's body to bury, only the fur-covered blanket upon which he had lain while recuperating from his fight. I buried his blanket and built a stone cairn. A day later, I returned with a slab of sandstone upon which Julie and I had engraved the following:

BATIAN
July 1988–July 1991

He was only three years old when he died.

It was nearly a year later, after his killers had been found guilty of illegally shooting Batian and had received paltry fines, and after much cajoling of insensitive South African nature conservation officials for his remains, that I finally brought Batian to rest in the Tuli bushlands. One afternoon, Julie and I went to the stone cairn and I buried my Batian's skin and skull. I am inflicting upon myself great grief in writing these words, but write I must to make known the cruel and senseless killing of lions that persists throughout Africa, lions shot for 'sport', for man's pleasure. It is happening as you read these words.

After Batian's death, I would sit each afternoon beside the cairn of stones. I would question the value of my work. Despite this work, Tuli lions were again being killed. I could not prevent the killing of one lion, my lion, by man. It was, however, beside Batian's grave that one day I received an answer to my questions.

One evening, before returning to her cubs, Furaha walked with me down to Batian's grave. As the western horizon glowed at sunset, I sat to one side of the cairn and Furaha the other. It seemed unusually quiet and I think we both sensed Batian's presence. A herd of impala crossed to the west but did not see Furaha and me. Furaha's head rose and together we watched them pass. Then, with their passing, we stood and slowly headed away in golden light.

The following evening, I went down to Batian's grave alone. Upon reaching the grave, I saw to my surprise lion spoor, and that of cubs, beside the cairn of stones.

The night before, Rafiki and the little ones had walked past the grave. I sat at the base of the cairn with the footprints of little lions around me. I touched the small pugmarks on the soft soil and my mood lightened. There, around me, was the answer to my questions. I was looking at the future; the future being living lions, little cubs and those of their kind yet unborn. I needed renewed courage to continue in my efforts for the lion and, as I sat there, I drew my courage from a remarkable lion called Batian.

CHAPTER

12

Darkness Dawning

> He has made a memorial for Batian and sits there most evenings. It is most heart-wrenching to see him go out through the gate, knowing he is off to be with Batian – and feeling only a fraction of what he must be feeling.
>
> Julie, from her diary

The evening walks down to the stone cairn became almost a ritual. While quietly leaving the camp, I would ponder deeply on what had occurred. On reaching the cairn, I would sit, cry a little, sometimes a lot, then later rise and walk away, strangely calmed, somehow strengthened.

Batian's death was reported upon extensively in the press, first in southern Africa and then in the media elsewhere. I did not want to talk about his murder, but I was compelled to do so. I had to – to highlight as much as possible the morally corrupt behaviour of his killers in the hope that by focusing attention on the way he died it would prevent other lions in the future dying as he did. It was a long-term message, however. The wish to kill, to achieve dominance over the lion, to bolster a strange kind of self-vanity by killing the Symbol of Africa are the deep-rooted attitudes of some men.

Batian's killers were unrepentant. They spoke to the press in callous tones. By so doing, though, by not denying they killed

Batian, they sentenced themselves before their trial even took place. The game-farm owner stated in an article: 'I'm not interested in sob stories and emotional crap. If I come across another lion busy catching or endangering my game, I'll shoot it.' In another report, he was quoted as saying: 'If I come across a lion in the veld, I don't say, "Listen, lion, just wait there. I'm going to [the] Nature Conservation [authorities] to get a permit to shoot you." I don't believe I have to.'

The game-farm owner and his manager were charged with hunting a lion without a permit, for not reporting what they had done and for illegally using bait (a donkey) to attract lions.

At this time, I spent hours at our phone on the banks of the Limpopo river answering questions from journalists, and as the media reported on what had occurred, the public became outraged. We received numerous kind letters from the public in South Africa, and internationally, expressing sympathy.

I tried to focus my efforts on the plight of the remaining Tuli lions still within the northern Transvaal and followed up on reports on where they had been seen. The exact number of lions was uncertain, but I knew for sure that two of old Darky's lionesses and three cubs were still surviving across the river. I proposed once again to the Transvaal Nature Conservation authorities that the remaining lions be darted and brought back to Botswana. I was informed by them that I must have the full agreement of the landowners on whose land the lions were before they, the authorities, would agree to my proposal – the landowners being the man who had shot Batian (who agreed to the move) and the De Beers company who owned the Venetia Game Reserve. Venetia's conservation management would not agree that the lions should be moved back to Botswana for they wished to keep the lions in their reserve. (Prior to this time, resident lions had been extinct in that portion of the northern Transvaal for over fifty years.) Venetia's management's attitude and views I felt were self-centred. Basically, as a new enterprise, they wanted the lions in their reserve because they would represent one of the prized 'Big Five' (which comprises lions, leopards, buffalo, elephant and rhino). They could not, though, provide the lions with total protection and because of this I felt that they could not have been working in the best interests of the lions. I became frustrated when they informed me that they would not agree to my proposal, but they did add that predator-proofing would be erected on their reserve's boundaries to prevent the lions from wandering on to lands where they could be shot and where killings had already taken place.

I was concerned about what would occur in the short term as predator-proofing cannot be established overnight and at any time, the lions could find themselves outside the Venetia Game Reserve.

Only three weeks after Batian's death, what I feared for the lions became reality. 'Rancher shoots two more lions – this time Batian's killers get a Permit', read a newspaper article. Incomprehensibly, the Transvaal Nature Conservation authorities had issued Batian's killer with permits to shoot two lions. I heard that the game-farm owner had come across five lions at a water-hole on his land and was 'charged by one of the animals and forced to shoot', according to the Chief Director of Transvaal Nature Conservation. Batian's killer had been granted the permits 'because predators posed a serious threat to livelihood', despite my calling for the lions to be safely relocated back into the Tuli. I was enraged.

The Chief Director was also quoted in the press as saying that my proposed darting and relocating of the lions was not feasible as it was extremely difficult to locate them [the lions], because they moved over vast distances'. This was incorrect – the lions were, after all, used to vehicles, approachable, could be tracked and in my view could feasibly be darted. Prior to the fresh killing, I had warned the conservation authorities that if either of the adult lionesses were shot the cubs would also die, unable to fend for themselves. Despite my warning, the authorities issued the permits.

Batian's killer shot and killed one lioness and it was reported in the press, 'that the other [lioness] was wounded, apparently crawling away through the bush to the sanctuary of the De Beers game ranch'. He shot the lioness with the full blessing of the Nature Conservation authorities.

I was now up against the conservation authorities, Venetia's conservation management (because they had refused to agree to the lions' removal) and the attitudes of people within the Tuli.

A manager of one of the largest tourist game-lodge operations in the Tuli, whose business is surely in part dependent upon lions as a tourist attraction, went on record saying, 'The whole issue, I think, is influenced by emotionalism.' These words were ironically similar to those uttered by Batian's killer at the time, who dismissed the reaction to the latest shooting also as 'emotionalism'.

Batian dead, a lioness allegedly 'run over', another shot dead, another wounded, cubs now orphaned and both game-lodge management and Batian's killer using the same word, 'emotionalism', as if it had distasteful connotations. 'What is wrong with caring? Who are the conservationists?' I asked myself angrily. I was once again facing the smug, 'pragmatic', cool-blooded attitudes that prevail so much in sectors of the conservation world in South Africa. Additionally, I was not receiving support for my proposal to relocate the lions back into the Tuli by some of the Tuli landowners. There was generally a lack of support from within. They were strangely quiet during that period. Perhaps they were being diplomatic since at that time, they were negotiating with De Beers for the sale (and driving by helicopter) of Tuli elephants for reintroduction into the Venetia reserve.

Statements made publicly by some South African conservationists were as cool-blooded as those coming from the northern Transvaal and the Tuli. An executive of the South African Wildlife Society (which has an extremely high number of members from the public) was quoted as saying that he could understand the reasons behind the issuing of the permits and noted in a very damaging generalisation that, 'Lions are not an endangered species.' He said in a newspaper report, 'Although it is not pleasant to see lions killed, I think the authorities handled the matter in a very responsible way.' Ironically, just prior to the killings, in an editorial dealing with the subject of 'problem animals' published in the Wildlife Society's magazine, it was concluded that if the indiscriminate killing of predators continued, it may well prove that the ultimate problem is man himself. I felt as though I was looking through Alice's looking-glass.

If you wish to see the legacy of the 'very responsible way' in which the sickening affair was 'handled', visit the taxidermist shop in the little town of Alldays in the northern Transvaal. There you may see a 'mounted' lioness. Price? R9,000. This lioness, who was one of old Darky's lionesses, mother to his cubs, a lioness with whom Batian later associated, died like him. Once this lioness freely roamed the moonlit plains of the Pitsani as her ancestors did. Today, she is dead. Today she is a bizarre facsimile created by man, a facsimile which depicts her not as she was, but how some man perceives her and her kind.

History was grimly repeating itself. Five years previously, when the Tuli lions were being killed in a similar fashion, a lion I had known since it was two weeks old was shot like Batian and the others and displayed in the same taxidermist shop. At that time, I wrote the following:

> Its face had been moulded into a fearsome snarl, its body stiff and misshapen . . . while a shell of a lion can be given a price, a living lion is surely priceless. It seemed strange that a masterpiece created by man, an ancient sculpture, for example, is revered by him as a holy relic. However, a masterpiece created by Nature, a lion, a form of life much older than the human race, is still today destroyed for pleasure. Such is the strange way of some men.

These heartfelt words were but an echo of the past, an echo of what George Adamson had felt and wrote of thirty years previously. He had written:

> One evening we came on a magnificent lioness on a rock, gazing out across the plains. She was sculptured by the setting sun, as though she were part of the granite on which she lay. I wondered how many lions had lain on the self-same rock during countless centuries while the human race was still in its cradle. It was a thought which made me reflect that although civilised man has spent untold treasure on preserving ancient buildings and works of art fashioned by the hand of man, yet he destroys these creatures which typify the perfection of ageless beauty and grace. And he does so for no better reason than to boast of a prowess achieved by means of a weapon designed by man to destroy man.

As the weeks passed, the controversy continued. The Director of Transvaal Nature Conservation and I were brought together to debate the issue on South African television. The two interviewers had, I felt, anticipated an angry fight and at times our discussion did become heated. What the debate basically highlighted was our differing attitudes towards the role of predators and our differing views on the whole game-farm industry. The Director stated early on that the lion had run out of '*Lebensraum*' – living space – but because of the establishment of 'game farming' there was more wildlife around than in the past. He seemed to indicate that his department's main role was to satisfy the game farmers, stating when questioned that at times both cheetah and wild dogs, two of Africa's most threatened predators, are also destroyed because of conflict with game farmers.

I agreed that the lions' present range in South Africa (and the range of other large predators) was but a fraction of what it was two hundred years ago, but I emphasised that although game farming was replacing cattle farming, it should be recognised that, like his predecessor, the game farmer does not welcome nature's predators. He sees them in the same light as the former cattle farmer – a threat because of the economics of an industry which publicly portrays a 'conservation' label. I stated additionally that small fenced game farms are often unviable in the ecological sense, the wild animals being unable to move freely and without the essential role of the predator being allowed to be played out. These and other factors reflected that game farms were often mere facsimiles of the true wilds – a subject I will write of later in this chapter.

When tackled on why his department had issued Batian's killer with permits to shoot more lions, the Director said the decision to do this was taken after full consultation with all neighbouring game farmers, etc. This I felt was quite untrue, for if Venetia's management had been consulted on the issue, they would have objected strongly, since they obviously wished the remaining lions to survive, preferably in their own reserve.

The Director also stated that when issuing the permit, a consideration had been that Batian's killer claimed that a giraffe had been killed by lion on his land – a giraffe is 'worth' R7,000 in the game-farm industry. I doubted the validity of this claim. Giraffe had been absent from the Tuli for almost a century before being reintroduced some nine years ago. Despite the giraffe population increasing with time, Tuli lions had never preyed upon them. I asked, therefore, why Tuli lions crossing into South Africa would suddenly begin to prey upon giraffe?

When the Director was questioned about why the lions had crossed into South Africa, he said that they could have been influenced by the introduction of 'foreign lions', that is my lions, into the Tuli. In reply, I said that unnatural man-induced factors, luring and baiting for example, were the reasons why the lions crossed into South Africa. What else would resident and stable lionesses of the Lower Majale pride, who had lived in an area of high density of prey all their lives, suddenly be motivated to leave their core area and enter an area of higher human activity, disturbance and less prey availability?

The real debate started when the television discussion ended, and it took place in the foyer of the studio building. I shook, as did Julie, who was with me, when the Director began making uninformed statements on not only the lion issue, but the Tuli area generally. I suppose that his words were a form of release to him, now speaking in an unofficial capacity. The scene was that of a government official, normally restrained by government dictum, letting off personal steam.

Our views could not have been more contrasting – and were worlds apart.

Batian's death exposed, and continues to do so, a sector of game farmers who generally hide behind their conservation mask, but who are in fact the real enemies of predators. The game farmer could in turn become his own worst enemy. With South Africa emerging from its political isolation of the past, game farmers, conservationists and conservation authorities must remove their blinkers and look ahead holistically. The indiscriminate killing of what should be naturally occurring predators in game areas will not be accepted by the public in Western countries – the potential tourists to South Africa. Unless there is a change in attitude and outlook, with publicity this factor within game farming, along with other aspects of the game industry, could prove to be damaging to the game farmer. The game industry could be recognised internationally as bloodthirsty and money hungry.

Some seventy thousand game animals are helplessly caught up in the game industry every year. Aspects of this industry have already attracted criticism. For example, the conditions animals have to endure at game auctions cast doubts over the true motives of the 'conservationists', who insist that wild animals 'must pay their way', or, to use their other phrase, 'If it pays it stays'.

Just after Batian's death, the results of an in-depth investigation into the South African game industry were published by a popular magazine. The findings of the investigation were shocking and

153

created a public furore. It was stated that, 'South Africa's pride in its noble game heritage is becoming a ghastly nightmare.' Game animals are captured from the wild, transported to the game auctions, held in pens, then sold and transported to totally new surroundings. In the investigation, it was reported that of one 'load' of game animals worth some R75,000, only a single animal, a zebra, survived rehabilitation at its new destination. Other horror stories were reported: half-starved gemsbok antelope with skin hanging over their ribs in holding pens, unable to adapt to feeding in captivity; the female zebra that had miscarried and had the afterbirth still hanging while it stood in the pen. No veterinary attention was given to her. The story of the white rhino which was bought, transported to a game farm, turned loose, but was still so drugged that it could barely stagger, let alone walk or run away from the aim of the game farmer's hunter-client's gun.

It was also reported that during transportation from a game farm, blesbok had their legs tied so tightly together with nylon stockings that circulation was cut off and several of the antelope had to be put down. In addition, more than fifty per cent of springbok are lost due to capture and translocation stress. The investigation concluded: 'The game industry as a whole must accept that if it is to continue without public outcry, guidelines for capture and transport must be implemented.' True words, but these are just some aspects needing attention in an industry which morally needs to clean up its act.

The whole concept of utilisation of wildlife on private lands needs to be rethought, to become holistic in its approach. Game farmers with their small fenced areas need to be educated that ecosystems are more likely to be destroyed when divided and carved into small units. If fences were dropped and private conservancies formed, wildlife would be allowed essential greater free movement. Predators could be reintroduced to perform their important predatory role and maintain their intricate relationship with the species upon which they prey. Large conservancies can support the tourists' Big Five and benefits from 'ecotourism' would be accrued by the landowners and surrounding communities. Paradise would not be lost but portions of true Africa would be reformed and rediscovered.

Dr George Schaller clearly illustrated the predator's essential role, and ultimately how all life around the predator benefits, when he wrote:

Predators are the best wildlife managers . . . The predators weed out the sick and old, they keep herds healthy and alert. The beauty of antelope, their fleetness and grace, their vital tension, are the evolutionary products of a constant predator pressure that has eliminated the stolid and slow. Man, one hopes, has gained wisdom from his past mistakes to realise that, to survive in all their vigour and abundance, the prey population need the lion and other predators.

In the troubled time after Batian's death, returning to the Tawana valley, Rafiki, Furaha and the five cubs were Julie's and my strengthening ray of hope and inspiration. It was at this time that Julie wrote the following, and what she writes sums up the story of the Last of the Free.

Gareth and I returned to camp after spending a few days away. We were both hot, tired and dusty from the seven-hour journey and Gareth had been worrying about his pride whom he had not seen for ten days. (Although this demonstrated their complete independence, one cannot but worry about them – especially after Batian's death.)

We drove past our sign, 'Tawana Camp – No entry without prior permission', and trundled along the kilometre-long track which leads to our home. As we rounded a bend just before the camp's entrance, we saw Rafiki nearby in the bush. We stopped at the gate, which Gareth opened then closed as I drove in.

As I got out of the vehicle and looked back towards Gareth and Rafiki beyond the gate in the bush, I was greeted by a most uplifting sight. As I watched, I couldn't help but feel so proud of Gareth, so happy for his pride – all the effort, trauma and literally blood, sweat and tears were rewarded by those few moments which told a complete story.

Gareth bent down rubbing his head with Rafiki as she moaned her greeting. From the bushes behind them, Furaha trotted towards Gareth with her characteristic determined stride, intent on saying her hello too. Both lionesses rubbed themselves against Gareth's legs, pushing themselves towards him and competing for his attention. I looked on from within the camp, and beyond the trio, in the scrub behind them, five smaller tawny forms peered from beneath the bushes – and nervously one by one crept forward. Gradually, and with utmost caution, the cubs continued although they soon settled on the old fallen boughs of a leadwood tree, their legs dangling and tails twitching.

It is almost impossible to describe adequately in words the picture that the pride with Gareth formed. Typical of a Tuli evening, the night was golden and soon Furaha, Rafiki and Gareth sat together contentedly while the little faces of the cubs peered over and under the branches of 'their' tree.

An atmosphere of absolute contentment pervaded and it was a moment which I consciously etched into my mind as I battled with my own emotions.

Then the Chief Captain came, and said unto him, 'Tell me, art thou a Roman?'

He said, 'Yea.'

And the Chief Captain answered, 'With a great sum obtained I this freedom.'

And Paul said, 'But I was free born.'

Acts 22: 27–8

AUTHOR'S NOTE

The story of the Adamson lions and the Tuli bushlands is still being lived . . .

And so I deliberately closed this book with the time of Batian's death. I felt this tragedy marked the end of a portion of the saga I shared and continue to share with Julie, with lions, in the bushlands.

Of what was to come later, there is much to write, and so I am preparing a sequel to *Last of the Free* – to tell of what was to unfold over the two often dark years following Batian's death, and what is still unfolding today in the life of the Last of the Free.

If you wish to know more about the Tuli Lion Trust – a trust dedicated to the conservation of the lion in the Tuli bushlands and throughout Africa – please write to:

The Tuli Lion Trust
c/o Ernst & Whinny
PO Box 41015
Gaborone
Botswana
South Africa

It has been expressed in the past that my writings could be negative for tourism in the bushlands. I disagree, particularly in the case of *Last of the Free*. For the bushlands it is my hope that *Last of the Free* becomes a valuable platform to promote this wonderful but little known wilderness.

I do believe though that in term and practice 'Ecotourism' should replace 'Tourism' in the bushlands. Ecotourism to me is the interdependence of Tourism, Conservation and rural communities. Today in the bushlands the owners of the Tuli Safari Lodge and I have have launched the 'Born to be Free Experience' – an ecoventure from which parts of the proceeds are put aside for conservation projects in the Tuli bushlands.

SHADOWS OF GOLD AND GRAY
A VIDEO DOCUMENTARY

Lion Man of Africa, Gareth Patterson, lives among shadows of gold and gray, among the lions and elephants in an African wilderness called Tuli. In this documentary, you are invited to enter Gareth's world, meet his lions, share his intimate relationship with them, and accompany him as he searches for his lost Rafiki. Along the way, become acquainted also with the life of the African elephant, as Gareth tells of those great herds - mighty symbols of liberty in this harsh land.

In *Shadows of Gold and Gray*, you will share Gareth's grief and outrage over the human threat facing his beloved lions and elephants, as he clearly points out the desperate need for greater protection of the Tuli Bushlands and those who dwell there. Share also his hope as he describes how the local Tswana communities can become part of a new philosophy of conservation for this wilderness. Learn how a program of eco-tourism could be an essential tool for the mutual benefit of all Tuli inhabitants, while helping to ensure that these magnificent creatures do not become shadows of the past, but remain a living presence in the land for generations to come. (57 Min.)

To order a copy of this video, send a check or money order made out to "**kinetic e**" in the amount of:

$49.99 for each video ordered.
plus **$ 4.99** postage/handling per video ordered
plus **$ 3.62** sales tax per video ordered (7.25%- *Texas residents only*).

Orders will be shipped via U.S. First Class (Priority) Mail. Please allow four to six weeks for delivery. Mail orders and/or address any inquiries to:

SHADOWS OF GOLD AND GRAY
kinetic e
P.O. Box 93093
Austin, TX 78709

∎

Part of the proceeds from sales of this documentary will benefit the **Tuli Lion Trust**, established by Gareth Patterson and dedicated to the preservation of the lion and all the inhabitants of the Tuli Bushlands. For more information, or to make a welcome donation, please write to: "The Tuli Lion Trust," c/o Ernst & Whinney, P.O.Box 41015, Gaborone, Botswana.